What Is on the HOME IMP____ CD-ROM?

MW00445953

With the CD-ROM accompanying this book, planning your home improvements can be even easier! The CD includes dozens of demos, shareware programs, worksheets, databases, and other helpful tools designed to make your house a home with less expense and hassle. Also included is $15 of free online time on CompuServe—the most popular online service in the country.

You'll find over 35 shareware and demonstration programs, 12 worksheets and databases, and graphics files of sample layouts, all designed to help you improve your home in the following areas:

- Planning Improvements
- Designing and Building Your Home
- How-To Help
- Garden and Landscape
- Safety, Security, and the Automated Home
- Financial Improvement

In the chapters of HOME IMPROVEMENT, you'll discover ways to use these programs to make your home improvement nightmares seem like simple tasks. (See Appendix A for full descriptions of these programs.)

In addition to all this, we've included WinCIM, the software you need to access CompuServe in Windows, and a connection to CompuServe via ZiffNet.

System Requirements

- 386DX-33 (486DX-33 or faster recommended)
- 4MB RAM (minimum)
- 4MB available on hard drive
- Super VGA adapter (supporting 640-by-480 resolution and 256 colors) highly recommended
- Microsoft mouse or 100-percent compatible
- Microsoft Windows 3.1 or higher

What it's on the HOME IMPROVEMENT
CD-ROM?

→ MS-DOS 3.0 or higher

→ Single-speed CD-ROM drive (double-speed recommended)

See Appendix A for instructions on how to use the CD-ROM that accompanies the book.

HOME
IMPROVEMENT:
Total Planning on
Your Computer

Home Improvement: Total Planning on Your Computer

Alan Neibauer

ZIFF-DAVIS PRESS
EMERYVILLE, CALIFORNIA

Copy Editor	Kelly Green
Project Coordinator	Cort Day
Proofreader	Nicole Clausing
Cover Illustration and Design	Regan Honda
Book Design	Regan Honda
Technical Illustration	Sarah Ishida and Cherie Plumlee
Word Processing	Howard Blechman
Page Layout	Tony Jonick
Indexer	Anne Leach

Ziff-Davis Press books are produced on a Macintosh computer system with the following applications: FrameMaker®, Microsoft® Word, QuarkXPress®, Adobe Illustrator®, Adobe Photoshop®, Adobe Streamline™, MacLink®*Plus*, Aldus® FreeHand™, Collage Plus™.

For U.S. rights and permissions, contact Chantal Tucker at Ziff-Davis Publishing (fax number 1-212-503-5420).

If you have comments or questions or would like to receive a free catalog, call or write:
Ziff-Davis Press
5903 Christie Avenue
Emeryville, CA 94608
1-800-688-0448

ISBN 1-56276-334-2

Manufactured in the United States of America
10 9 8 7 6 5 4 3 2 1

To Barbara

Table of Contents

→ | *Acknowledgments*

I'd like to thank everyone at Ziff-Davis Press for their support in the preparation of this book, and for their foresight in creating this remarkable series of books. Thanks to publisher Cindy Hudson, acquisitions editor Suzanne Anthony, and editor Kelly Green.

I am also grateful to all of the shareware authors who graciously gave their permission to include their software on the CD-ROM packaged with this book. These include Roger Altman, Dannis Austin, Stephen Billard, David R. Black, Gary R. Buhler, Martin Butcher, Bruce Christensen, Larry E. Fosdick, Jeffrey L. Gates, Anjan Ghose, David Grimmer, Bill Hammond, Paul Hartman, Chuck Herndon, Richard Holler, Steven Hudgik, Gayle Y. Hughes, David Huras, Michael D. Jones, Philip P. Kapusta, Steven W. Leiphart, Fred S. Lindow, Robert Scott Mace, Robert A. Mace, Don H. Norman, Boyd W. Penn, Paul Postuma, Fred Schipp, and Carl Wegman.

You probably spend more time in your home than anywhere else. It takes the largest percentage of your money. You cannot live without it. And just like a person, your house needs some TLC. It must be maintained and cared for, repaired when something breaks down or just wears out. Major and minor improvements will make your home more comfortable, easier to maintain, and more in tune with your lifestyle and tastes.

But maintaining a home can be quite complex. Just think of the heating, plumbing, and electrical systems; the roof, walls and floors; and kitchens and baths. Your home has thousands of parts, and any one of them can break or go bad.

This book will help you use your computer to maintain and improve your home. With your computer, you can learn how to make repairs and improvements yourself, or find out how to evaluate and hire contractors to do it for you.

Can your computer really help? Here's just one example. A friend of mine wanted to add a small addition onto her house. She was on a tight budget, as most of us are. By studying several home improvement computer programs, she felt that she could so some of the work herself—installing the electrical wiring, laying a hardwood floor, and installing the insulation and paneling. She designed the addition and then hired a contractor just for the major construction. She finished the room herself, using step-by-step guidance that she found on computer programs and over an online service. While the project took a little longer than expected, she saved more than $1,500 by doing some of the work herself.

While you may not be planning such a major project, you too can use your computer to save money, to ensure that the correct work is completed, and to get that satisfied feeling that you did it yourself. Your computer—and this book—can help you accomplish it.

In Chapter 1, you will learn why you should use your computer to improve and maintain your home. You will find out how to connect to online services and how to evaluate the resources that are available to you.

Chapter 2 focuses on planning home improvement projects. You will learn how to estimate the materials that you'll need for a project and how to finance and budget major improvements.

In Chapter 3 you will learn how to design and lay out an improvement project—from a small renovation to a major addition. You'll also learn about computer programs that use three-dimensional graphics to let you see your completed home before you even begin.

Getting detailed how-to help is covered in Chapter 4. There is no need to experiment or go through trail and error when you can learn professional techniques and tips on your computer. Learn how to use tools, select materials, and make repairs.

Chapter 5 is all about kitchens and baths, two of the most expensive rooms of your house. You will learn how to plan these rooms and how to design their layout.

Do you enjoy working in your garden or just relaxing on your deck or patio? Chapter 6 is devoted to your garden and landscape. You will find out how to learn about plants, create a pleasing landscape, grow vegetables, and even build a deck.

Chapter 7 is about safety, security, and home automation. First you will learn how to take a complete inventory of your home. Then you'll learn how to automate your home's lighting and security systems. You can even have your computer turn on your coffeepot in the morning and turn off your house lights when you go to sleep at night.

Appendix A explains what you'll find on the CD-ROM and how to use it. The CD contains many of the shareware programs described in the book. So not only can you read about these programs, you can start using them right away. The CD also contains all of the worksheets and databases illustrated in the book. You'll find the worksheets in both Excel and Lotus 1-2-3 formats, and the databases in Access and dBase formats. In Appendix B, you will find out where to get more information about the programs discussed throughout the book, both commercial and shareware.

1

Your *Home* and Your *Computer*

Your

home is perhaps one of the most expensive purchases you will make, and it consumes the largest part of your income. This is true whether you are a do-it-yourself person or you hire other contractors to work for you—whether you are buying, renting, or leasing a home or having one custom-built for your family.

A home is much more than a shelter. It is a part of the family, a safe haven. To make your home feel comfortable and fit into your lifestyle—and to keep it that way—you should make decisions about your home carefully, using the best resources available.

Your computer can provide you with these resources. Using software and on-line services such as America Online, CompuServe, and Prodigy, you can benefit from the experiences of others—homeowners as well as contractors and other professionals.

➔ Your computer as a home resource

Your computer can provide the resources you need to design, improve, and maintain your home.

Throughout this book, you will learn how to use your computer to plan, design, maintain, and improve your house and garden. The focus will be on these key areas:

- ➡ Using your computer to plan your home's overall design and layout. Multimedia programs let you select a home design and modify it to suit your own tastes.

- ➡ Using your computer to plan the details and layout of kitchens, baths, and rooms. Computer software lets you design rooms and even "walk" through them in virtual reality.

- ➡ Using your computer to plan and perform home improvement and maintenance projects. You can get expert advice, and even step-by-step guidance, from professionals.

- ➡ Using your computer to plan your garden and landscaping. Software is available that lets you plan the layout of individual plants and trees, and you can get professional landscaping advice online.

- ➡ Using your computer to track your home's contents. You should keep good records of your possessions for insurance and estate planning purposes.

- ➡ Using your computer to control your home's electrical and security systems.

- ➡ Using your computer to get how-to advice and determine whether to do the job yourself or call in a professional.

In many cases, you can use software that you already have for these activities. So if you are on a budget, you may not have to purchase expensive software to take advantage of the techniques discussed in this book. You can use a spreadsheet program, such as Excel or Quattro Pro, to perform most of the calculations and computations, to keep track of inventory and expenses, and to help plan improvement projects. You can use a drawing program such as Paintbrush, which comes free with Windows, to sketch improvement ideas, drawings, and floor plans. You can even use the drawing function of word processing programs, such as Word for Windows and WordPerfect for Windows, for your most basic tasks.

If you find these programs to be limited, however, then you'll need to consider signing up with an online service or buying additional software. Fortunately, most of the programs described in this book are relatively inexpensive.

Finding Information Online

Subscribing to an online service—such as CompuServe, America Online, or Prodigy—makes home-related information just a phone call away, although the resources available depend on the service. Online services charge a monthly fee that allows you to get online for a specific number of hours or to access certain information free of any additional charges. There may be extra charges to access some features, to find more extensive or technical information, or to connect for time beyond the basic hours provided.

Chances are you will not select an online service just because of its home information. If you only have the budget to subscribe to one service, carefully evaluate your options before making a decision. All of the online services offer a wide variety of information, games, and programs, as well as the opportunity to communicate with other members. Most allow access to online encyclopedias and magazines, current news stories, weather information, and sports reports. You can transfer software programs directly from the service to your own computer in a process called *downloading*.

You can also share your thoughts with other service members. Forums and roundtables let you send messages to and receive messages from other members. In fact, the online services have hundreds of forums, each dedicated to a specific interest, such as a hobby or profession. There are also chat services that let you communicate in real time. Chatting is like talking on the telephone, except you type your message on the keyboard rather than speaking. You may also join an online service to access electronic mail or to connect to the Internet.

To connect to an online service you'll need a modem. Your computer may already have a modem built in—many computers, especially laptops and notebook computers, come with fax-modem boards installed. If not, you need to purchase either a modem card or an external modem. Modems are relatively inexpensive. You can purchase a basic no-frills fax-modem starting at around $60. More expensive modems have special features, and they allow your computer to communicate with the service at faster rates.

When you shop for a modem, consider its speed. While faster modems might cost a little more, they transfer information quicker. If your service charges you for time spent online, the higher modem cost is more than compensated by reduced service charges. Modem speeds are given in baud rate or bits per second (bps), two measures of the speed by which information can be carried. While these measurements are not technically the same, they are often used interchangeably. You should not consider a modem with a speed less than 2,400bps. If your budget allows, consider a modem with a speed of 9,600bps or 14.4kbps (the fastest of the three).

You might also consider purchasing a fax modem. Not only will you be able to join an online service, but you will also be able to send and receive faxes directly from your computer. The price difference between a fax modem and a modem without fax capabilities is negligible.

➜ Making the online connnection

To connect online, you need a modem, cable, and communications software.

A modem card fits inside your computer. Installing the card is easy, but it requires that you open your computer and carefully follow the manufacturer's instructions. If you are uncomfortable delving into your PC's interior, then have the card installed where you purchased it. An external modem sits outside of the computer. You use a cable to connect it to your computer's serial port.

You'll need to connect your telephone line to the modem. Place your computer near a telephone jack, or run a phone extension wire from the jack to the modem.

Your best online sources for home information are America Online and CompuServe

You'll also need communications software, which lets you and your computer communicate with the service. When you sign on with the service, you must choose a password; this ensures that no one else can sign on using your name and accumulate large online charges. Depending on the service, you get a password either the first time you sign on, or on the phone through a service representative.

Throughout this book, you'll learn about resources the popular online services can make available to you. In this chapter, we'll compare five of the most popular services—CompuServe, America Online, GEnie, Prodigy, and Delphi. All of the services make the sign-up process easy, and all have toll-free telephone numbers where you can get help and assistance.

Most of the online services offer a free trial period. In many cases, you pay no basic fee for the first month, although you may have to pay for any services that you use that are not included in the monthly rate.

Your best online sources for home information are America Online and CompuServe. Home options from GEnie, Prodigy, and Delphi are rather limited, although Delphi offers complete access to the Internet, as you'll learn later.

With Prodigy, get information from the Money and Finance section of Consumer Reports—choose the Housing/Real Estate option. You can also try the Homelife Bulletin Board, or you can contact any of commercial services that advertise across your screen. Prodigy charges a basic monthly rate of $9.95 for unlimited use of "core" services, but bulletin boards and some other options cost an additional $2.95 per hour. To connect to Prodigy, you'll need special software supplied by the company. You can purchase a Prodigy Start Up kit at most computer stores—you may even get it free with your computer or modem. The kit comes with the software on disks and a password that lets you get started. After you install the software, you can connect to Prodigy using the password provided and complete the sign-up procedure online.

Get information about housing and real estate on Prodigy.

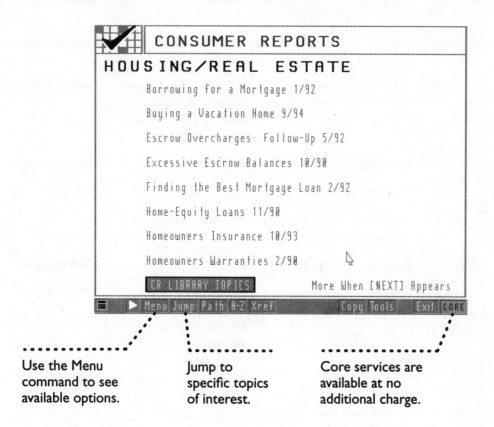

CONSUMER REPORTS

HOUSING/REAL ESTATE

Borrowing for a Mortgage 1/92

Buying a Vacation Home 9/94

Escrow Overcharges: Follow-Up 5/92

Excessive Escrow Balances 10/90

Finding the Best Mortgage Loan 2/92

Home-Equity Loans 11/90

Homeowners Insurance 10/93

Homeowners Warranties 2/90

CR LIBRARY TOPICS   More When [NEXT] Appears

► Menu Jump Path A-Z Xref   Copy Tools   Exit CORE

Use the Menu command to see available options.

Jump to specific topics of interest.

Core services are available at no additional charge.

If you have GEnie, your best source of information is from the Home and Real Estate Roundtable, or from some of the other discussion groups. GEnie has a monthly service charge of $8.95, with an additional fee of $3 per hour for non-primetime usage after the first 4 hours. There is an additional $9.50-per-hour charge for primetime connection—Monday through Friday from 8 a.m. to 6 p.m. You can use any communications program to connect with GEnie—the program

Table 1.1

Comparing Five Online Services

Service	Monthly	Additional Hours	Terms	Contact
America On-line	$9.95	$2.95	5 hours free each month, no extra charges	1-800-827-6364
CompuServe	$9.95	n/a	Unlimited use of standard services, with $4.80 per hour for extended services	1-800-848-8990
Delphi	$10.00	$4.00	4 free hours	1-800-695-4005
	$20.00	$1.80	20 free hours	
	$3.00 for Internet		No extra charges	
GEnie	$8.95	$3.00	4 free hours	1-800-638-9636
Prodigy	$9.95		Unlimited use of core services, with $2.95 per hour for non-core services	1-800-776-3449

that comes with your modem, the Terminal accessory that comes free with Windows, or the communications facilities in OS/2. To sign on to GEnie, you use your modem to dial a toll-free number and then complete the sign-up process online. You select your password when signing up.

Delphi has a large number of special interest forums, such as Home Improvement and Repair, Hearth and Home, and Plant Lover's Forum. In addition, Delphi offers complete access to the Internet. Delphi has two billing options. The 10/4 plans gives you 4 hours of free non-primetime services for $10 per month. The 20/20 plan gives you 20 hours a month for $20. Additional charges apply to prime time connections, and Internet access costs $3 per month. Extra time is charged at $4 per hour. You can use any communications program to sign on and use Delphi.

America Online has three main areas for home information:

→ Real Estate Online Forum offers professional advice, a listing of homes for sale around the country, access to mortgage companies, and software to download.

→ Homeowners Forum offers news of interest to homeowners, home improvement information, and a message board and chat area to contact other members. You can also join the United Homeowners Association to access additional information and to get discounts on travel and home products.

→ HOME Magazine Online offers searchable contents of the magazine, professional advice, house plans and layouts, software to download, and a message board.

America Online has a monthly fee of $9.95 to cover the first 5 hours of on-line time. After that, you pay a $2.95 hourly connect rate. America Online provides its software for free. In fact, you may find the software packaged with a magazine, or even receive it in the mail as part of a promotion.

CompuServe is a very extensive network that offers three types of services: basic, extended, and surcharged. You can use the basic services all you want without accruing any charge in addition to your $9.95 monthly service fee. For extended services you pay an additional $4.80-per-hour access charge. Extended services are listed with a plus sign on any CompuServe menu. All forums and bulletin boards are extended services, including the two you'll find most useful for planning your home:

→ Dwellings Forum provides information, software, and a message board covering every aspect of home ownership and repair.

→ Family Handyman Forum offers software and a message board on home repair and maintenance.

America Online's HOME Magazine Online

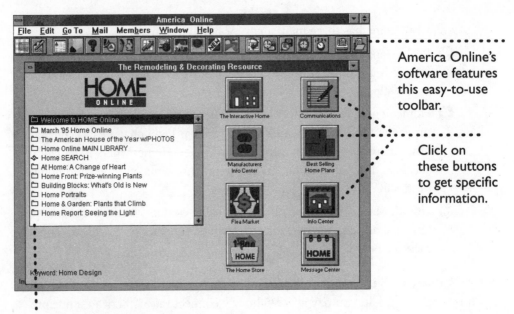

America Online's software features this easy-to-use toolbar.

Click on these buttons to get specific information.

The menu offers easy access to services and information on a variety of topics.

Surcharged services charge an additional fee that is added on to your monthly CompuServe bill. These are indicated by a dollar sign on the menu. The surcharged services are operated by other companies, but they use CompuServe as the means of connection. Sometimes the fees are based on your time online, such as charging additional amounts for each minute connected. So while CompuServe might not be charging you for the online time, the service is. In other cases, you only pay a surcharge when you ask the company to perform a certain service, such as mailing you a research article or looking up information in its database.

CompuServe's extended and surcharged services provide research tools for both the consumer and the professional researcher. While surcharged services cost a bit more, they provide extensive capabilities. For example, the ZiffNet area

The Dwellings Forum on CompuServe

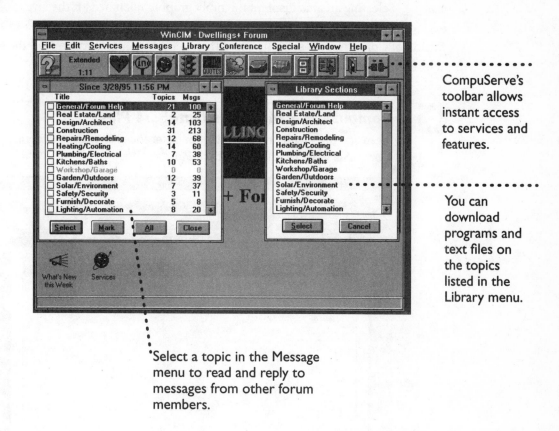

CompuServe's toolbar allows instant access to services and features.

You can download programs and text files on the topics listed in the Library menu.

Select a topic in the Message menu to read and reply to messages from other forum members.

provides access to Ziff-Davis magazines, such as *ComputerLife*. Magazine Database Plus is a surcharged service containing articles from hundreds of publications. Searching the database is charged as an extended service—you only pay a $1.50 surcharge to read or download an article. It is an excellent way to find information not available elsewhere on CompuServe, or information so current it has not yet been updated onto other services.

You search the database by entering a key word or phrase. If a search results in a large number of matches, you can refine the search by looking at subdivisions or related topics. Shown below, for instance, is the result of searching for the phrase *house buying*. Clicking on subdivisions under House Buying breaks down the 270 citations into 37 areas, such as *contracts*, *economic aspects*, and *financing*. Selecting an area displays the bibliographic reference for the articles. To read a specific article, select its check box (or click on the reference with a DOS version of CompuServe's software), and then click on Read. To download the article, click on Retrieve.

 ## CompuServe's Magazine Database Plus

Here are the results of searching for references to *house buying* in CompuServe's Magazine Database Plus.

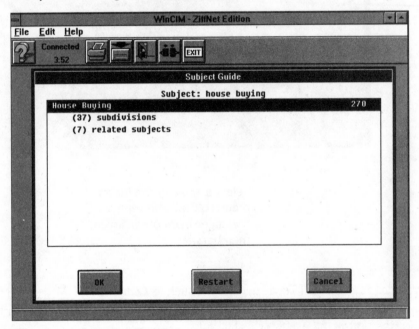

Because the surcharge is not applied until you read or download the article, take your time and search the database thoroughly. If you get a long list of articles, download the references without charge by selecting Save from the File menu. You can then study the list at your leisure offline and download specific articles later using the reference number from the main Magazine Database Plus menu.

You can use any communications program to connect with CompuServe, although CompuServe works best with its own software, which you can get for free.

For the adventurous, there's the Internet. The Internet is a network of thousands of computers in universities, government agencies, corporations, and community groups around the world. Finding and getting information on the Internet can be a real challenge and often frustrating. You can spend quite some time following a path to a source, only to find that it requires a password or is not available.

You can connect to the Internet through CompuServe, America Online, Prodigy, and Delphi, although the range of Internet services offered varies. You can also sign up for the Internet through any number of national or regional services, called Internet providers.

Using the Internet is much easier if your provider has a gopher service. A gopher is a series of menus from which you select options. You do not need to know the specific address of the Internet source or how to get there, you just select an option to display an additional menu or to log-on to an Internet node.

Both America Online and Delphi offer extensive gopher menus. Delphi, however, is the only service that offers unlimited access to all Internet resources. From the Delphi gopher you can access other gophers and services throughout the world.

For example, suppose you are planning to relocate to Saint Paul, Minnesota. Since many communities offer public access Internet resources (called freenets), you decide to search the Internet for information about community resources in that area.

Using Delphi, you would first select the Schools, Community Resources, and Freenets option from the main gopher menu. Another menu appears with the option Freenets and Community Access. Choosing that option displays a list of freenets across North America. By selecting City of Saint Paul, MN, you get access to the Saint Paul library system, a community calendar, and other local resources.

For those interested in the Internet, there are numerous guides listing gophers and other Internet resources. For general lists of Internet resources, look on your online service or bulletin board for the Desktop Internet Reference (d_10inet) or the Internet Guide (IPWIN.HLP).

As an alternative to commercial online services and the Internet, consider using local bulletin boards. These are run by individuals, schools, or user groups for the benefit of the community. Most are free, although you may need to join a user group for some access. A *user group* is a group of people who get together monthly to share their interest in computers. These groups charge a nominal membership fee. Some user groups also sponsor annual computer sales, training sessions, and conventions. Bulletin boards do not offer the research and reference features of online services, but they do put you in touch with other homeowners like yourself. They are an excellent way to find out about area contractors and get recommendations and advice.

To find bulletin board numbers, ask at neighborhood computer stores or go to computer swaps, shows, and user group meetings. You may also find them listed in community newspapers. For a definitive source on bulletin boards, get a copy of *Boardwatch* magazine in your local bookstore. The magazine is a reference for finding, using, and establishing bulletin boards.

Using local bulletin boards can be quite an adventure. You may be on your own in making the connection and learning how to set up your communications software. In most cases, you can use any communications program, including the Windows Terminal accessory or the terminal program that came with your modem. Try connecting using the default settings when you first run the program. If you have trouble connecting, your software settings probably do not match those of the bulletin board.

In order to communicate through a modem, your software must be using settings similar to those used by the bulletin board. Your software will have some menu option or command to change these settings. You will see options to change the baud rate, the number of digital bits that make up each character, the type of system your software uses to detect errors—called parity—and the number of digital bits transmitted after each character. If you can, call the bulletin board over a regular voice line and ask the representative how to set your software. (For example, you may be told to set your system at 2400 baud, 8 data bits, no parity, and 1 stop bit.) Look at your software manual, or go through its online help system to learn how to adjust the settings.

Local bulletin boards are generally uncontrolled (unmonitored), so you'll never know about the quality of the advice, of any programs that you may download, or of the etiquette of others using the service. Use an antivirus program to check out downloaded software, and avoid giving out your address or phone number.

Software for Your Home

If you can't find what you want online, you can bring a complete library into your home through software. Unfortunately, evaluating software can be rather complex. Every program offers something a little different, making it difficult to recommend one over the other. New software is constantly being released, and updates are being made to current programs.

You need to evaluate software based on your own skill level. Most room layout programs, for example, require some degree of practice and ability. You do not need to be a trained draftsperson, but do you need to understand how the program works and how to use its available tools and features.

Similarly, while programs can show you how to do something, and some can even tell you how to do it if your computer is equipped for multimedia, they cannot do it for you. You still need the tools and the manual dexterity to complete the job on your own.

This doesn't mean that you shouldn't bother to learn how things are done if you plan on hiring a contractor. On the contrary, you should learn as much as possible about the job. Knowing about the project will help you plan what you want done, it will help you discuss the proposal with the contractor, and it will help you evaluate the bid and the completed project. Learn what materials or parts are needed for the project, their costs, and the quality of work that you should expect. Find out how the contractor should proceed and any special warning signs that you should look for to determine whether or not you are getting what you pay for.

Your software selection will depend on your hardware, your budget, and your information needs.

The software you choose depends on the features of your computer's hardware. You'll find a list of the minimum recommended requirements somewhere on most software packages. "Minimum requirements" refers to hardware and other software that you need to run the program. If you don't have the minimum requirements, and do not plan to buy the software or hardware required to meet them, then don't buy the software.

You may also see the recommended requirements needed to run the program listed on the software box. These are the hardware requirements that the manufacturer feels you'll need to run the program satisfactorily. If you meet only the minimum requirements, the program may not run very fast or smoothly, or not all of its features may be available.

Take the following features into account as you evaluate your hardware's capabilities.

➡ Is the program designed for DOS, Windows, or the Macintosh? Most, but not all, multimedia programs require Windows.

➡ How much memory is required? You'll need at least the minimum recommended amount. You can always add additional memory, but it can cost hundreds of dollars.

➡ How much hard-disk space is required? Don't assume that you can use your last free disk space for the program. Some applications take up additional space only when they run. Even if you have a little space left after installing the program, the available space may not be enough to use your applications.

➡ What size floppy disk is the program supplied on? Most programs come on 3½-inch disks, some come with 5¼-inch disks as well. Make certain that the supplied disk will fit in your computer. Many programs supplied on 3½-inch disks include an exchange certificate. If you need 5¼-inch disks, return the certificate and the manufacturer will send you the program on that size disk. Just remember that you can't use the program until the disks arrive.

➡ Does the program require a CD-ROM drive? If you do not have a CD drive then you can't use a CD-ROM product, no matter how wonderful and complete it is, so look for programs supplied on floppy disks. Many of the programs discussed in this book are available on floppy disk.

➜ Does the manufacturer recommend a double-speed CD-ROM drive? Most programs that do can still be used on single-speed CD drives. You'll usually be able to display, read, and print information, but movies and animated displays may appear slow and jerky. With a few programs, however, a slower drive will make the program run so slow that it will be virtually unusable.

➜ Does the program require a sound card for multimedia presentations? Do you need a headset or a set of speakers and a suitable cable? If you do not have a sound card you probably can still use the program, but you will not get the full effect of multimedia.

➜ What is the recommended resolution and the number of colors? Most programs require at least VGA resolution. Many recommend VGA or Super VGA with 256 colors. To get this number of colors, you'll need special video drivers that are usually supplied with your computer or video card. In some cases, you will be able to use the program even with the standard VGA setup; you just may not see as much detail in the graphics. In a few cases, however, multimedia movies will not run unless you have the 256-color Windows drivers.

Make certain that the software you buy contains the information and functions that you really need. Don't be swayed by dramatic multimedia presentations that you may view once, or show off to impress friends. CDs full of house designs are interesting, but may not be useful if you want to create your own design.

We'll look at the different types of programs and what they offer in later chapters. Study the programs carefully before you purchase them. Read the product descriptions and ask the computer store for a demonstration.

You may also be able to find shareware or public domain software to help you. Public domain software is absolutely free—you can use and copy it as much as you want without charge. Shareware is distributed for free, or for a nominal charge, but you are required to pay a registration fee if you decide to continue using the software after you've tried it out. For the fee, however, you usually receive the most recent copy of the software, and you often receive printed documentation and support.

The CD that accompanies this book contains many of the shareware programs that you will read about in the following chapters.

You can also download public domain software and shareware from online services, the Internet, and bulletin boards, or you can purchase it at local stores and by mail order.

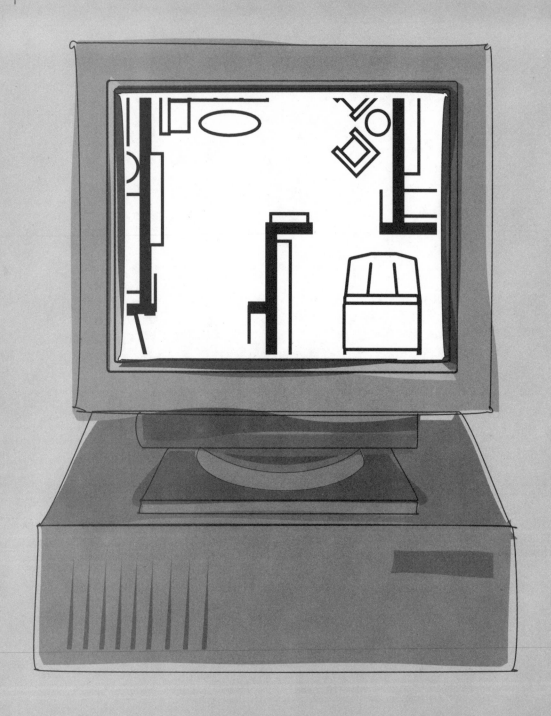

2
Planning Home Improvements

While

we may only purchase one or two homes in our lifetime, most of us are constantly maintaining or improving our current house, condominium, or apartment. It seems that there is always something that needs fixing or replacing, or that we'd like to add shelves or an addition or make some other improvement.

No matter how handy you are around the home, your computer can help. Your computer can be an excellent resource, almost as valuable as a knowledgeable neighbor or friend with the tools and know-how you need for your improvement project.

In this chapter, you will learn to use your computer to

➡ Design your home improvement project

➡ Estimate materials that you'll need

➡ Budget your project

➡ Plan home improvement financing

Designing Your Project

Don't skip the planning stage, even if you are just performing a small repair job. A mistake can turn the smallest repair into a major and costly renovation. Start by defining your needs, expectations, and the overall budget. Write down a description of the project, outlining the major steps you'll need to follow.

You should also plan an estimated time schedule. This is particularly important when a project involves a kitchen, bath, or other important room that will be out of service during the remodeling. Make certain that you can do without the use of the room, or that you can make alternative arrangements.

The Windows Calendar accessory is a convenient way to plan your time schedule. You can display it in day view, showing the details of each day in hourly increments. For an overview, change to month view. While you cannot add notations in Month view, you can mark days by selecting from five symbols: [], (), o, x, and _. Use the symbols to indicate major milestones, such as the delivery of materials or the demolition of a wall. Add the details of the schedule in Day view.

Use Windows Calendar to schedule your project

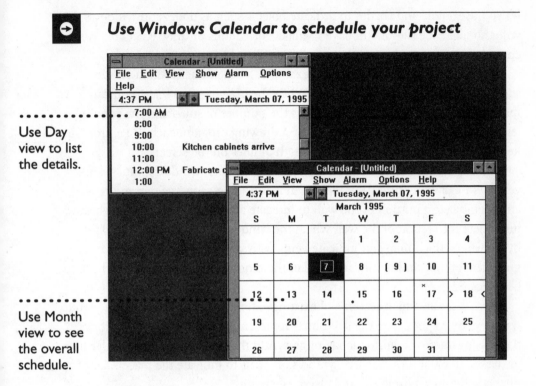

Use Day
view to list
the details.

Use Month
view to see
the overall
schedule.

Start by defining your needs, expectations, and overall budget

Sketching Your Project

Design your improvement project before you start it. If you are planning an addition or major renovation, use a CAD (computer-aided design) or layout program, which you'll learn about in later chapters. For a quick sketch of your project, however, you can use Windows Paintbrush or any other drawing program.

Start by measuring the existing walls and drawing them in the layout. You may want to begin by drawing a rough sketch on paper. When it looks correct, redraw it using a program such as Paintbrush. A computer drawing program will let you use colors and shades to indicate objects such as doors and windows. It will also make it easier if you have to make corrections or draw it accurately enough to show a builder or designer.

Try to draw the plan to scale. For example, let each quarter-inch on the screen represent a foot of wall space. When the drawing is to scale, you can more quickly calculate materials such as the number of studs and the running length of pipe and wire. If you are using a drawing program such as Paintbrush, keep a ruler handy and measure the length of lines on the screen.

Use the drawing tools to mark the location of doors, windows, pipes, and vents. For example, indicate a door by drawing a line at an angle from the wall and then delete a portion of the wall to indicate an opening. To show a window, just delete the section of the wall where the window would appear. Show pipes by drawing a thick line, and indicate vents with small rectangles. You'll save a great deal of time and money if you plan the room so these items do not have to be relocated.

Next, indicate which sections of existing exterior or interior walls you plan to remove. You might delete the solid lines representing these walls and redraw them using another color or shade of gray. Add the new walls using a wider line or darker color, and then insert symbols or labels to indicate the placement of appliances, fixtures, plumbing, and electrical circuits.

Use dimension lines to show the length of walls. A dimension line indicates the size of a wall or the spacing between objects. For example, you should add dimension lines to indicate the placement of doors, windows, appliances, fixtures, and outlets. If you're using Paintbrush or another drawing program, add dimension lines using the line tool and note the sizes of walls and other distances with the text tool. Use small circles to indicate electrical outlets—place a letter *s* in the circle where you want a switch.

Making Measurements

It is a waste to order supplies that you may not be able to return. Planning, designing, and laying out a project will help you determine the materials that you'll need to purchase.

➡ **Sketch your project before starting it.**

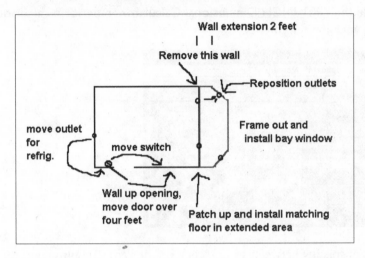

In order to accurately estimate the amount of materials you will need, you must carefully measure the square footage of the project area.

If you use a tape measure to take measurements, you may record dimensions in feet and inches. But you cannot multiply feet-and-inch measurements on a regular calculator to compute square feet. One solution is to convert your feet-and-inch measurements to all inches or into decimal—30 inches or 2.5 feet instead of 2 feet 6 inches. Better yet, you can use a calculator that lets you enter measurements in feet, inches, and even fractions.

If you use Windows, install the Mini FEET INCH Dimensional Calculator from the CD packaged with this book. This shareware program from Claw Software displays a calculator much like the one that comes with Windows. However, you enter measurements in feet and inches, and you can also input fractions of inches. The program converts the measurements to decimal for performing the calculation.

Now suppose you are paneling a room with a perimeter of 15 feet 7 inches and you need to determine how many studs to buy. Enter **15** in the calculator and then press Enter. Next, click on **7** and then press Enter. This enters the measurement *15ft.7in*. Now click on the division (÷) button. To designate 16 inches

Make calculations easier.

Use the FEET INCH Dimensional Calculator to perform calculations on your measurements.

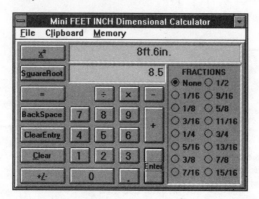

(the amount of spacing between studs), click on the zero (0) button and then press Enter to indicate no feet. Next, enter **16** and click on the equal (=) button to perform the math. The program calculates the result as 11.68753. Round up the result to 12, and then add one additional stud for the corner. So you'd need to purchase 13 studs to complete the wall.

For a DOS calculator program, look for the program Footcalc in the Repairs/Remodeling section of CompuServe's Dwellings Forum. You'll find it in the file FTCAL2.ZIP (46,084 bytes).

Using the Estimator Worksheet

The amount of materials you'll need for many interior projects depends on how much area in square feet is to be covered with paint, wallpaper, or wallboard. It will be easy to calculate the coverage area if you use a spreadsheet such as the one shown here. You'll find this Microsoft Excel worksheet, ESTIM.XLS, and a corresponding Lotus 1-2-3 worksheet, ESTIM.WKS, on the CD accompanying this book.

Use a worksheet to estimate materials.

	Microsoft Excel - ESTIM.XLS						
File **Edit** **View** **Insert** **Format** **Tools** **Data** **Window** **Help**							

Arial 10 B I U $ % 100%

A1

	A	B	C	D	E	F	G	H
1								
2		Feet	Inches	Total Inches				
3	Height:	0		0				
4	Length:	0		0		Number of walls:	0	
5	Width:	0		0		Number of walls:	0	
6								
7	Ceiling (1 or 0)	0						
8		Square Feet				MINI SQUARE FEET CALCULATOR		
9	Door Openings (sq.ft):						Feet	Inch
10	Windows (sq ft):					Length =	0	0
11	Other Subtractions (sq ft):					Width =	0	0
12	Other Additions (sq ft):					Square Feet =	0	
13								
14	Total Square Feet	0						
15								
16	PAINT							
17	Number of Coats:	0						
18	Coverage/Gallon:	0						

Sheet1 / Sheet2 / Sheet3 / Sheet4 / Sheet5 / Sheet6

Ready

Record the height, length, and width of the room. The worksheet lets you enter the feet and inch measurements in separate cells, and then it calculates the size in inches.

Next, enter the number of walls you want to cover in the Number of Walls column. If you are renovating the entire room, for example, you'll indicate two rooms for the length and two rooms for the width. In the cell beside Ceiling (1 or 0), enter 1 if you want to cover the ceiling, 0 if you don't.

Then, calculate the total square feet occupied by doors and windows. Since these areas will not need to be painted or wallpapered, you can save money by not including them in the area to be covered. Measure and multiply the height and width of each opening, and add the results of each to calculate the total door and window space. Notice that the worksheet contains a section that calculates square feet of an area when you enter the length and width in feet and inches. Either use these cells to compute square feet or use the FEET INCHES Dimensional Calculator.

Finally, measure and enter the square feet of any other wall or ceiling areas that you want to exclude in the Other Subtractions column, or that you want to add to the coverage area in the Other Additions column. For example, you may want to leave a section of wall as it is, or paint or wallpaper a closet to match the room.

Once you've entered all of your measurements, the worksheet calculates the total square feet of coverage. The worksheet uses this result to compute the amount of materials you need.

With paint, you enter the number of coats you want to apply and the square feet covered by one gallon of paint. You can find the coverage area on the paint can label. The worksheet multiplies the square feet by the number of coats, and then divides the result by the coverage per gallon.

Calculating the amount of wallpaper to use is just as easy. First, find out how many square feet each roll of wallpaper covers. Standard rolls cover either 28 or 36 square feet, depending on their manufacturer, so ask your dealer. When you enter the number into the worksheet, it determines the number of rolls by dividing the total square feet by the per-roll coverage.

The amount of drywall is calculated automatically using the square feet of coverage. The worksheet simply divides the square feet by 32, the coverage of one 4-foot-by-8-foot sheet.

You can calculate insulation in two ways, by square feet or by linear feet. For a quick calculation by square feet, look at the label on the insulation to find out how many square feet a roll will cover. When you enter the amount into the worksheet, a formula divides the number of square feet by the size of each roll.

As an alternative to using square feet for estimating insulation, you can calculate using the number of linear feet. The package around each roll will tell you its length. On the worksheet, enter the length of the roll and the distance between your studs. The worksheet divides the linear length by the distance between studs, and then divides the result by the length of each roll. The distance between studs is used to calculate the actual linear feet of coverage by eliminating the area covered by the studs themselves.

Always round up your estimates; 3 gallons of paint when an estimate reports that you'll need 2.7. You can usually return unopened cans of paint and rolls of wallpaper if you find you don't need them. Although you may not be able to return custom-mixed paint or special-order wallpaper, it is best to err on the plus side. If you purchase too little, you may have trouble finding the exact same item. Anyway, extra paint is useful for touching up or repainting. Also remember that there will be some waste when you wallpaper, especially when you have to match patterns, so it is best to order an extra roll.

If you do not want to calculate the materials yourself, there are numerous programs that do it for you.

Building: Material Estimators, from Books That Work, is a complete software package that estimates these materials:

- Lumber
- Concrete
- Drywall
- Paint
- Wallpaper
- Tile

For electrical work, it will tell you the recommended wire gauge, the size of junction boxes, and the size of the power supply your home should have. It will also calculate how much it will cost to run an appliance, and it can estimate the appropriate amount of attic venting.

For interior estimates, you first enter the perimeter of the walls and the ceiling height, the ceiling and floor areas, and the number of doors and windows. The program calculates the total number of square feet, using standard window and door sizes. You then specify additional details, such as the type of wallpaper and the condition of walls. The program estimates the amount of supplies you'll need. If you are installing drywall, for example, the program reports the number of panels and nails, the length of seam tape, and amount of mud compound needed.

Icons appear at the bottom of some screens to display additional information. For example, the By The Book icon gives tips about local building codes, the

Rule of Thumb icon shows general formulas and guidelines, and the More icon presents reminders about easy-to-forget details.

There are also shareware programs that help estimate required materials. *Handyman Conversions* is a DOS program for estimating construction materials for carpet, paint, cement, wallpaper, insulation, and roofing. Is also contains a fraction-to-decimal conversion chart, screens explaining how to compute perimeter and area, and a how-to section on measuring for insulation and roofing.

You'll find this program on the CD packaged with this book; run HANDY.EXE to install the program files on your hard disk. Once the program is installed, run HANDYMAN.EXE. Select the type of estimate you want from the main menu and then follow the prompts that appear on screen. For instance, if you select the paint estimator, you will be asked to enter the length and the width of the room, the height of the walls, and the number of doors and windows. Handyman will calculate the number of square feet and the number of gallons of paint required for one coat.

If you do not have a CD-ROM player, you can download the program from both CompuServe and America Online. On CompuServe, look for the file HANCON.ZIP (47991 bytes) in the Repairs/Remodeling section of the Dwellings Forum. In America Online, download the file HANDYMAN.ZIP from the Home Management library section.

Carpenter's Dream, another shareware program, provides a series of material estimations and calculations. Download the program WORKHORS.ZIP (242139 bytes) from the Home Management library of America Online, or the file WORKHO.ZIP from the Repairs/Remodeling section of CompuServe's Dwellings Forum.

The program calculates cubic and volume estimates for concrete and other materials, as well as linear and square options for decks, squares, and sheets. Several options perform calculations for cutting rafters, stairs, doors, and window openings. There is also an option that displays 55 useful tips about construction specifications. Graphic screens are used to illustrate the terminology used for stairs and posts, roofs, and rafters. You can enter measurements in decimals or fractions.

If you prefer using a spreadsheet program, download from CompuServe *Jovin's Home Remodeling and Small Contractor Templates* for Lotus. You can find the templates under the name HOMTEM.ZIP (54768 bytes) in the construction library of the Dwellings Forum. This is a series of Lotus 1-2-3 worksheets you can use to estimate for these materials:

- Concrete
- Framing
- Windows, doors, and stairs with interior trim
- Stucco
- Exterior siding
- Drywall
- Roofs
- Insulation
- Painting
- Modular kitchen cabinets and bathroom vanities

Some of the templates were created on a very early version of Lotus 1-2-3 for DOS. If you cannot open them in Lotus 1-2-3 for Windows, use the Lotus Translate utility to convert them to a newer format. You can open the templates in Excel. While the macros will not work, the formulas will still be calculated.

Planning Your Budget

Once you plan your home improvement project, you should determine how much the project will cost. If you are hiring a contractor, get two or more bids. Most contractors will give you a free estimate. Write down all of the specifications you receive in the contractor's estimate. Be sure to specify which items are included, and which you will have to purchase yourself or pay extra to receive. You may find that a low bid might not include items that are provided for in a higher estimate. Add these additional costs to the low bid for a more realistic comparison.

If you are performing the work yourself, start by carefully recording the names and amounts of the items that you'll need to purchase. If necessary, add a description of items that require exact specifications.

To get the most from your budget, do a little comparison shopping. Print out a copy of the list, take it to two or more building supply dealers, and record the cost of each item. Be sure to consider the cost of delivery. If you cannot transport the materials yourself, you'll need to have them delivered. While some suppliers deliver for free, others require a minimum purchase or charge for the service.

If you are planning a large project with many materials, consider a computer program designed just for project estimation. Two of the most popular estimator programs can even directly obtain a list of the supplies you'll need from a CAD or layout program, as you will learn in the next chapter.

If you are planning a large project with many materials, consider a computer program designed just for project estimation

Estimator Plus for Windows from ComputerEasy and *Design Estimator* from Abracadata are almost identical programs. They are designed primarily to help contractors create bids and estimates. You create a pricebook, listing the name, description, and price of raw materials. You then select items from the pricebook, indicating the quantities of each, and the program calculates the extended and total costs. You perform "what-if" analysis by adjusting labor costs, markups, and material costs.

Both programs can import material lists created by FloorPlan Plus 3D and Design Your Own Home, two layout programs you'll learn about in Chapter 3. You design the layout and then export the list of materials to an estimator data file. Each item used in the layout appears as another bid item.

The programs come with several bids and pricebooks on disk that serve as samples to get you started. You can order professional pricebooks for every area, except heating and air conditioning, from SSB Corporation. You can also purchase upgrades that provide additional capabilities such as conversion of bid quantities to order quantities.

Compute the cost of your project.

Use an estimator program to compute the cost of your improvement project. Many estimator programs get a list of materials directly from your layout program.

Estimator programs import the materials from your layout program...

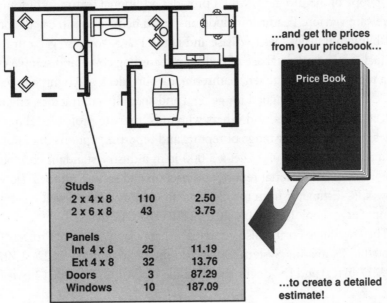

...and get the prices from your pricebook...

Price Book

Studs		
2 x 4 x 8	110	2.50
2 x 6 x 8	43	3.75
Panels		
Int 4 x 8	25	11.19
Ext 4 x 8	32	13.76
Doors	3	87.29
Windows	10	187.09

...to create a detailed estimate!

For shareware estimators, consider Remodel Estimator and PC-Estimator, both from CPR. *Remodel Estimator* is designed for estimating an addition, kitchen, deck, or any other home improvement project. A copy of Remodel Estimator is included on the CD accompanying this book. Use it to build an estimate and to create reports such as these:

- Estimate Summary
- Estimate Detail
- Trade Breakdown

➡ Estimate Identification

➡ Standard Costcodes

➡ Trade & Wage Listing

You can download Remodel Estimator from America Online's accounting library. Look for the file REMODEL.ZIP (138,144 bytes). Registered users get the latest copy of the program, which provides additional features not found on the shareware version. Features include on-screen help, a popup calculator, and the capability to transfer files to dBase and Lotus 1-2-3. You also get a printed users manual, a standard database of codes for recording costs, and sample estimates for a room addition, kitchen, bathroom, carport, deck, skylight, and garage.

PC-Estimator is designed for general and specialty contractors, engineers, architects, manufacturers, and others who must prepare professional quality estimates. It offers a wider range of reports and reporting options than Remodel Estimator. Registered users get a 3,000-item industry-standard costcode database file, a bill of material report, and backup and restore utilities. Download a copy of PC-Estimator from the construction library of the Dwellings Forum on CompuServe. Look for the file PCEST.ZIP (161,010 bytes).

The Dwellings Forum also contains a shareware version of ProDev*QUOTE Quote/Bid Estimating System. Download the program file PDQUO1.ZIP (309717 bytes) and the documentation file PDQUO2.ZIP (90013 bytes).

Over at CompuServe's Family Handyman Forum, look for these estimating programs in Library 12:

➡ ESTIMA.ZIP (129,901 bytes): Construction Estimator for DOS

➡ CONEST.ZIP (98,304 bytes): Construction Estimator 3.0

➡ CONSTR.ZIP (406,656 bytes): Construction Estimator for Windows

Financing Your Project

Major projects can mean major bucks! If you're not independently wealthy, you might need to finance your project by charging the expenses on a credit card, or by taking out a home equity loan. You could also consider a second mortgage.

Financing and mortgages can be a costly and time-consuming process, so you should get professional advice and assistance. Fortunately, there are many software programs that can give you this advice. These programs, for example, offer a wide range of home financing information:

- The Home Buyer's Companion (Parsons Technology)
- Buying A Home (FYI Software)
- Home Ownership Plus (Personal Vision)
- The Homebuyer's Guide (Books That Work)

There are also shareware programs dedicated to helping you make financing decisions. In fact, all of the following financing programs are included on the CD packaged with this book:

- The Mortgage Analyzer
- The Smart Homeowner
- QualifyR Windows
- Loan Qualification Excel Worksheets
- Amortization Excel macro
- Master Amoritiser
- Mortgage Designer
- Mortgage Calc
- House Mouse
- Loan Arranger

Once you take out an equity loan or second mortgage, you should carefully track your payments. You can use a general-purpose commercial loan program, such as Per%Sense from Ones and Zeros, to do this. You can also use the shareware program Home Loan Diary, by Philip P. Kapusta, which is included on the CD accompanying this book. Run LOANINST.EXE to install the program files onto your disk. To use the program, log onto its directory and run LOAN.EXE.

From the main menu that appears, select Begin New Loan. Enter the specifics of your loan and then save the information to your disk. As you make payments, start Home Loan Diary, retrieve the loan information, and then record your payments. You can also see how much money you can save by making additional principal payments.

By the way, if you are interested in buying a new home, considering a first mortgage or refinancing, install DREAMBUY.DOC from the CD accompanying this book. This Word for Windows file explains how to use your computer to determine if you qualify for a mortgage, to find a mortgage, and to locate and buy your dream house.

Financial Worksheets

In addition to the spreadsheet for estimating materials discussed previously, the CD contains two worksheets that you can use to plan your budget and finances.

- ➡ LOANQUAL.XLS will help you determine if you qualify for a mortgage. Enter the income and expense details requested, along with the principle, rate, and length of the loan.

- ➡ REFIN.XLS will help you decide about refinancing your mortgage. Enter the information requested about your current loan and the proposed refinanced loan. The worksheet will report how your monthly payments and total interest will be affected.

The Case of the Staggering Studs

Marc had always been handy around the house, so he decided to renovate his unfinished basement himself. This was the first time he had ever undertaken such a major project, so he carefully planned every detail. He estimated all of the materials that he'd need and went to his local building supply dealer. After pricing the individual materials, he was shocked by the total price. Marc then used Lotus 1-2-3 to create an itemized list of materials. He called a number of dealers to obtain prices for major items, such as wall paneling, studs, insulation, and ceiling panels. By entering the prices into his worksheet, he was able to determine the most inexpensive sources. While he had to purchase materials from two different dealers and pay for one delivery charge, he still came in several hundred dollars below his original estimate.

3

Designing and *Building* *Your* Home

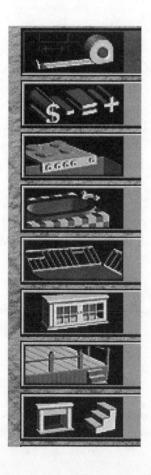

If you are building a new home or planning a major renovation to an existing home, then you should do some extra planning. Because of the complexities of new construction, you can use your computer to get professional advice and assistance for each step of the design and construction process. You can

- → Learn about home design and construction
- → Decide on the design and general layout
- → Select the type of construction
- → Design or modify your home's layout
- → Learn to work with builders and architects

Learning about Home Design

Before embarking on a major project, you should learn about the design process. You can learn quite a bit about this process through online services. If you subscribe to CompuServe, go to the Dwellings Forum and look at the Design/Architecture and Construction library sections.

If you subscribe to America Online, access HOME Magazine Online. Through the service's Interactive Home option you can access the Home Project Management Center, where you communicate with builders, contractors, and other homeowners.

Multimedia software can really help, too. The CD-ROM version of Broderbund's 3D Home Architect, for example, includes over 100 articles and 50 video clips on construction and remodeling. The articles, from *American HomeStyle* magazine, are organized into nine categories:

- → Planning, Designing, and Measuring
- → Value, Costs, and Vendors
- → Kitchens
- → Baths
- → Walls and Floors
- → Cabinets
- → Decks and Porches

➜ Stairs and Fireplaces

➜ Lighting

➜ **Use 3D Home Architect to learn about the design and construction process.**

In the Planning, Designing, and Measuring section, for example, you'll learn how to analyse your housing needs, and you will learn how to make measurements and read blueprints. If you are new to construction, you'll find the Value, Costs, and Vendors section particularly valuable. There you will learn how to specify building details and how to work with contractors to protect your rights and get a good finished product. The preconstruction checklist, for example, details each of the steps in the process—from finalizing the land purchase and blueprints to inviting your friends for a ground-breaking ceremony.

The program also includes a month-by-month list showing each of the major steps in the construction process. You can print out the list to measure your builder's progress. While you may have to adjust the timing for your own project and local conditions, the list of steps is useful for all home construction.

The video clips are narrated by Gerry Connel, host of "The Home Pro" on the Learning Channel. The clips explain important points to remember when designing a home, and they review some of the features of 3D Home Architect. The clips are best seen using a double-speed CD-ROM drive and a VGA video setup of 256 colors, and to hear them you'll need a sound board. You can view the clips with a single-speed CD-ROM drive, although the picture and sound may appear out of synch.

An alternative is Key Home Designer, a CD-ROM from Softkey, and its virtually identical twin, Complete House, from Deep River Publishing. The home design multimedia presentation of both contains four major sections:

- House Design
- Kitchen and Bath
- Magazine of Designs
- Resources

The House Design section is a tutorial on home design and construction. You'll learn the elements of a home, the considerations that go into the decision to build, and how to work with architects and builders. It also includes a nine-page home design questionnaire that will help you define your design goals.

Working with Builders and Contractors

By communicating with builders, designers, and other homeowners online, you can learn how to avoid some of the pitfalls that you can face when building or remodeling your home.

In the Homeowners Forum on America Online, select the Home Improvement option and then choose Builders, Architects, and Lawyers. There you can access a series of useful articles, such as:

➜ "How to Choose a Contractor"

➜ "Before You Sign the Builder's Contract"

➜ "Don't Lien on Me—Avoid Paying Twice for the Same Work"

In the Real Estate Online area, look for articles in the OurBroker section, such as "How to Pick A Builder," the file BUILDLTR.TXT (16,840 bytes), from JBS Publications.

On CompuServe, go to the Design and Architecture section of the Dwellings Forum. You can then download files such as "How To Find An Engineer"—file NSPE.TXT (8944 bytes). You'll also find a series of files provided by architect and designer Martin Butcher, two of which are included on the CD accompanying this book:

➜ What Should You Expect From Your Architect?—file MBWWYA.TXT (17,054 bytes)

➜ Finding The Architect Of Your Dreams—file MBHTFA.TXT (5,744 bytes)

Install the files from the CD and then open them into any word processing program.

In Prodigy, jump to the Homelife Forum. In the Building and Repair section you can access the Ask A Builder and the Ask a Contractor message areas for professional advice.

Finding a Home Design

Once you have a sense of your housing needs, start looking at home designs. While you'll still need an architect and builder, you can save time and money by planning ahead of time the type of home you want, its general layout, and the type of amenities that it should include. You can view sample house plans on your computer using software or online services.

Most of the layout programs that we'll discuss in this chapter include sample floor plans. One excellent example is Planix Home, a layout and design program from Foresight Resources Corporation. Included with the floppy disks that store the program itself, you get a CD-ROM that contains 500 floor plans and 20 house designs. You can supplement these by purchasing Most Popular Home Designs, a CD-ROM containing illustrations and floor plans for 200 homes. Most Popular Home Designs includes Home Finder, an easy-to-use search system that lets you select homes based on up to four criteria: style, number of bedrooms, number of baths, and square feet.

Most Popular Home Designs is one of many programs that lets you display three views for each home:

- ➡ *Plan view* displays the two-dimensional floor plan.
- ➡ *Birdseye view* displays a three-dimensional view looking into the building from above.
- ➡ *Rendering view* displays an artist's rendition of the home's exterior.

You can view sample house plans on your computer using software or online services

If you want to get home plans online, access *Home* Magazine Online on America Online. In addition to information on home design and improvement, you can download a monthly home plan. Each plan includes a full-color artist's rendering of the home, along with floor plans and a brief description.

➡ *Display three views of your home plan.*

You can access thousands of home plans using software or online services. Some even present three views, as shown here—Plan view, Birdseye view, and Rendering view.

Plan View

Birdseye View

Rendering View

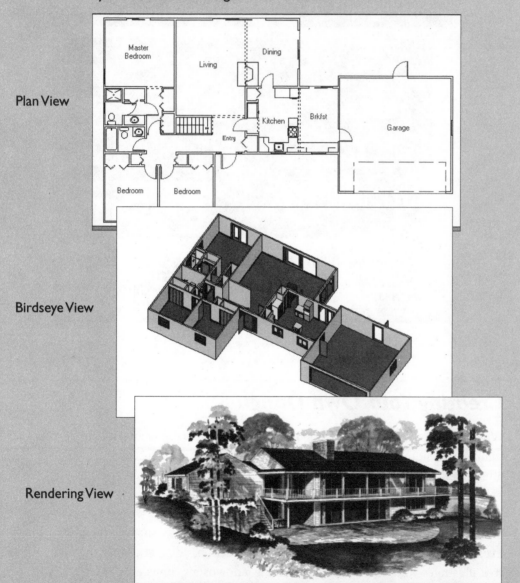

Home plans on America Online

Home plans from America Online's HOME Magazine Online include an artist's drawing of the house, floor plan, and a description. You can download a new plan each month.

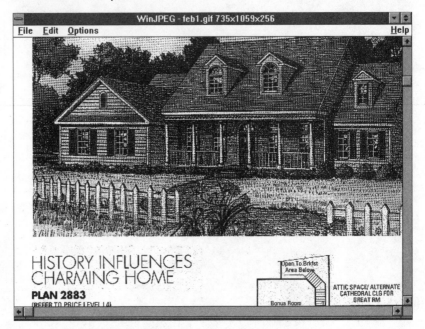

Creating Your Own Design

Whether or not you are a hands-on type, you should take an active role in designing your home or your home improvement project. This means that you must carefully study all designs or blueprints to ensure that the completed project will meet your expectations.

Your computer can help you take an even more active role. Using your computer, you can select a house design and then modify it for your own lifestyle. Even if you know little about design and construction, you can change the plan so it illustrates your goals, such as changing a downstairs powder room to a full bath, combining two smaller rooms into one, or expanding the size of closets. Your architect can then finalize the plan so it conforms to building codes and acceptable building practices.

With layout and design software you can take more creative control over the design of your home in these ways:

- → Design your own layout
- → Modify your architect's proposed layout to suit your needs
- → Plan the layout of furniture
- → Create shopping lists of furniture and appliances
- → Display three-dimensional views to visualize the completed project
- → Experiment with the position and color of walls, doors, appliances, and furniture

There are many programs that let you create floor plans and room layouts. Unless you're creating the simplest of plans, however, you will need to develop some skill to create accurate detailed layouts in the correct scale. Selecting a layout design program is a very personal choice. Your decision will depend on your needs—how detailed you want the drawing to be and how much time you want to spend creating it. For example, if you want to create blueprint-quality drawings, then you'll need a program that has CAD (Computer Aided Drafting) capabilities. CAD programs allow you to create precise drawings that contain the details needed by architects, builders, and building inspectors. You'll also need to spend some time learning the advanced features and techniques of CAD software. If you just want to arrange furniture in your living room, then you'll want a program that is easy and intuitive.

Here are some features to consider when evaluating programs:

- → *Snap-to-wall drawing* lets you easily create intersecting walls with neat corners.
- → *Auto-dimensioning* inserts dimension lines and measurements indicating the length of walls and the spacing between architectural elements.
- → *Three-dimensioal view* displays a virtual reality image of a two-dimensional floor plan.
- → *Symbol libraries* contain predrawn images of appliances, fixtures, and furniture. A good program will include a wide range of these symbols.

➡ ***Customize the layout to your own tastes and family needs.***

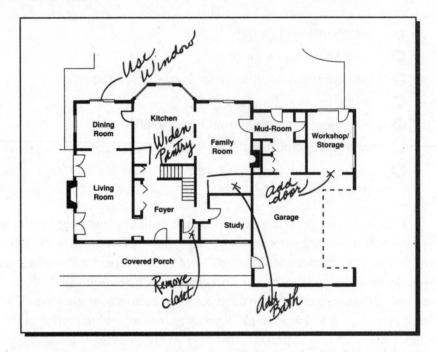

➡ *Architectural details* allow insertion of items required by architects, builders, and planning agencies, such as electrical wiring and foundation piers.

➡ *Reports* create lists of building materials, fixtures, and furniture needed to complete the project.

You might also want to consider a program's use of layers. Layers separate design elements into logical groups. Imagine each layer as a piece of clear plastic. You place one layer on another to visualize the composite plan.

Some programs, for example, let you use a separate layer for each floor (story) of the home. You can then superimpose the layers to check for layout problems such as placing a nursery directly above a potentially noisy family room.

Other programs use layers to store each category of objects—for example, one layer can contain exterior walls, doors, and windows; a second layer can contain interior walls; a third layer electrical symbols; a fourth layer landscape elements; and so on. You can then printout separate copies of each layer for each subcontractor.

Creating Your Home with Three Dimensions

We'll first look at several programs that provide three-dimensional capabilities. Three-dimensional imaging requires a lot of system resources. In some cases you'll have to wait up to several minutes for the program to convert the plan to 3D. Once the 3D image appears, it may take an additional delay each time you use the mouse or keyboard to change your position.

FloorPlan Plus 3D, from Computer Easy, provides three-dimensional views with CAD capabilities. The ends of intersecting walls automatically align into neat corners or junctures, and you can insert a dimension line along each new wall with a click of the mouse.

Its symbols are divided into seven areas:

- Appliances and fixtures
- Cabinets
- Doors
- Furniture
- Landscaping
- Miscellaneous
- Windows

You can choose between nine window styles, 22 doors, and 86 appliances and fixtures. The 50 landscape symbols include plants, trees, decking, fences, and other exterior objects. A wire and pipe tool and electrical objects allow complex architectural detail. The dialog box where you select symbols shows each in two- and three-dimensional views. The three-dimensional view even rotates to display all sides.

➡ *The art of layering*

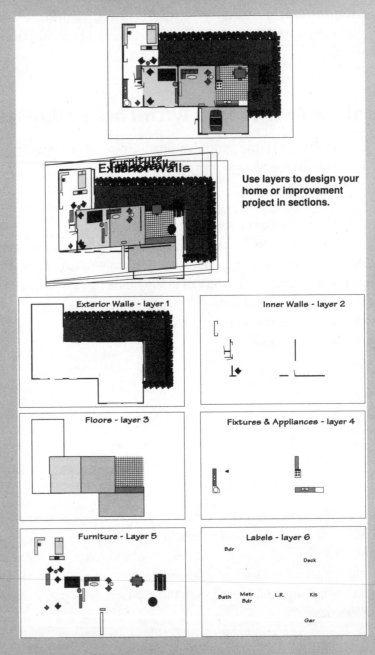

Use layers to design your home or improvement project in sections.

Exterior Walls - layer 1

Inner Walls - layer 2

Floors - layer 3

Fixtures & Appliances - layer 4

Furniture - Layer 5

Labels - layer 6

You can edit each symbol to customize how it appears on your plan, such as changing its length, height, width, distance off of the floor, and line and fill style. Other editable options depend on the object type. For instance, when you insert a handrail into a landing, you can edit the handrail width and thickness, the opening between balusters, and the handrail and baluster colors.

Each symbol has an associated part number. The numbers are used to create a materials list, which you export to a text file. The list itemizes each appliance, fixture, and furniture item in the drawing, as well as the number and types of doors and windows. It does not itemize other building materials, such as the number of studs, although it reports the total running lengths of interior and exterior walls and the square feet of roof. From these, a contractor can estimate building materials.

When you add an element to the layout, the program automatically places it in one of 13 predefined layers. For example, when you add a line indicating a wire or pipe, the line is placed in the wire and pipe layer. Doors, windows, walls, symbols, labels, and other elements are also placed in their own layers.

You can display all of the layers to view the entire drawing, or you can view selected layers. So, for instance, you can print the walls and wire and pipe layers for your electrician and plumber. A copy of just the walls and landscape layers would be useful to your landscaper.

In addition to layering elements of a layout, FloorPlan Plus 3D can accommodate up to 20 stories of a multiple-story building. When you add a new floor, the lower level of layers appears gray so you can easily coordinate the arrangement. You can select to display the floors superimposed or individually. This combination of layers and floors present an almost infinite number of combinations.

While the program is mainly designed for interior layouts, it also includes a unique roof editor for designing the exterior look of the building. The roof editor lets you design dormers, chimneys, and skylights showing side, top, and front views of the building.

Both the floor plan and roof editor images can be displayed in three-dimensional view. You select between wire frame and solid designs, and move around the image using the mouse or keyboard. (You can also switch to a DOS 3D viewer for faster response time, but it requires a lot of memory.)

A demonstration copy of FloorPlan Plus 3D is on the CD packaged with this book. The demonstration version has all of the CAD capabilities of the full program, except you cannot print or save your layouts, and it contains just 50 of the 300 symbols. You can still create detailed layouts, see your plans in three dimensions, and use the roof editor.

Before trying your hand at your own layout, take a look at a sample design. Choose Open from the File menu, and then double-click on one of the sample files ending with the .fp3 extension.

> ### Use FloorPlan Plus 3D's roof editor to help visualize your new home's roof.

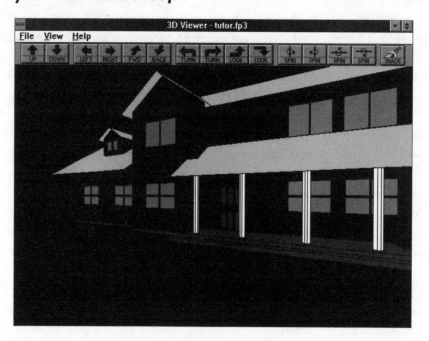

Broderbund's *3D Home Architect* also offers many CAD-like features. It includes drawings and plans for 150 homes, as well as a wide range of architectural symbols. You select objects from the toolbar or from a series of menus. Clicking on the door button, for example, will display five additional buttons showing door types. Click on the type of door you want and then click on the wall where you want to insert the door. The window, cabinet, and electrical buttons work the same way. Clicking on the fixture or furniture button displays the first of a series of menus. You select the type of item to display additional choices, sometimes moving through three or four levels to select the specific object to insert. You can edit the size of any of the built-in symbols to customize them for your layout.

The program offers some special features for convenience:

- ➡ The corners of rooms automatically align, forming perfect angles.
- ➡ You can drag the walls of a completed room to change its length or width.
- ➡ Dimension lines snap to a wall so you do not need to worry about exact placement.
- ➡ You can add dimension lines to all exterior walls with two clicks of the mouse.
- ➡ You can reverse the entire plan with two clicks of the mouse.

One of 3D Home Architect's most useful features is Plan Check. Plan Check reviews your layout, warning you of potential errors and code violations based on standard building practices—rooms without doors, stairs that do not reach the next floor, or a windowless bathroom without an exhaust fan, for example.

Once you complete your plan you can generate a thorough report of building materials—not just fixtures and furniture, but also the number and square feet of studs, joists, wallboards, and other materials. It will even give the running length of moldings.

While 3D Home Architect does not use layers, you can work with up to four floors and a foundation. You can quickly create a new floor using the walls of the lower level as its template, or you can design the new floor independently.

The program provides four views:

- ➡ Two-dimensional plan view
- ➡ Two-dimensional elevation (front) view
- ➡ Three-dimensional overview, a birdseye view of the entire structure
- ➡ Three-dimensional eye-level camera view

~🖳~

If you prefer a DOS interface without the overhead of Windows but still want 3D capabilities, then consider *Home* from Autodesk. Autodesk Home is a solid CAD tool with extensive symbol libraries, including one containing objects for disabled users.

With Autodesk Home, you can also select from seven types of flooring materials, six types of siding, and two types of roof materials. All of the symbols are available in both feet/inches and metric units, and in plan and elevation orientation. You use the elevation symbols to create a two-dimensional front view of a room or wall. You create a layout in plan view and then change to 3D view for either an eye-level or birdseye overview. Once you design your layout you can generate a shopping list of electrical items, fixtures, appliances, and furniture.

Using Two-Dimensional Layout Programs

Three-dimensional views are interesting and can be quite useful, but they are not always necessary. If you are not interested in three-dimensional capability, then consider a program that provides only two-dimensional layouts.

Key Home CAD, for example, is easy to use, it comes with 20 sample files, and it can create excellent floor plans. It lacks some of the details and features needed for blueprint quality, but it does include 12 complete symbol libraries. You can change the size and color of symbols and you can create your own symbols using drawing tools.

Each plan consists of up to six layers. You control the number of layers displayed, and you can name the layers to indicate their contents, such as exterior walls or furniture. Key Home CAD is identical to the CAD floor plan layout program supplied with Complete House.

Design Your Own Home Architecture, from Abracadata, comes with 24 complete plans, and it includes 11 symbol libraries. You can create up to nine layers, dimming lower levels while you work on the active layer. You can also view a base layer that represents everything in the combined layers. If you delete a layer, objects on it are added to the base layer. So you can delete a layer while retaining its contents. Because the layers are not already defined according to their contents, you can choose to use them for individual elements or additional floors as you desire.

Doors, windows, and trees are supplied on both plan and elevation perspective. Use elevation views to create a interior or exterior view. Symbols in the fences library are all elevation, as are columns from the miscellaneous library.

Some special features in Design Your Own Home Architecture include:

- ➜ A stud tool for specifying the number of each type of stud to purchase
- ➜ Dimension lines that snap to the wall
- ➜ Lists of building materials and objects
- ➜ Ability to export the materials list to an estimating program

Planix Home is a complete CAD-quality program for home and landscape design. It makes creating a basic layout easy using the Shell dialog box. You select from six basic shell designs and then enter the outside wall dimensions. Planix automatically draws the exterior walls for you. You can later modify the design by adding, deleting, and changing walls, but the shell saves you the trouble of dragging individual walls for the basic shape of the home. While walls do not automatically snap together for neat corners, you can later select the walls and use a corner command to clean up the intersections.

Planix comes with 21 extensive symbol libraries that let you create complete blueprints. For example, the wire symbol library contains details such as the wiring of three-way electrical switches. The documentation includes a printed listing and picture of every available symbol. There is even a separate symbol editor program for creating and modifying symbols.

Selecting a symbol is easy. You click on a toolbox button to list common symbols in its category, or you click on the button for a dialog box listing all available options.

Planix includes 22 predefined layers, one for each type of object that you can add to your plan, as well as 14 reports listing details or summaries of building contents.

Designing Your Home with Shareware

If you want to experiment with home design before investing money, consider a shareware layout program. Shareware programs do not have the full range of features that you'll find in commercial software, but they provide many of the basics. Two shareware layout programs are supplied on the CD that accompanies this book, one for DOS and one for Windows.

HomePlan is a DOS program where drawings have the look of blueprints. While it lacks the easy interface of Windows, it provides a number of special features:

- Automatic dimensioning
- Optional display of framing studs and joists, spaced either 16 or 24 inches apart
- Allows for reversal of the entire plan either horizontally or vertically
- Square Footage Calculation
- Measurements in either metric or feet and inches

When you run the program, select *HomePlan* Tutorial from the main menu to learn more about the program, or select Load a Plan from Disk to open sample plans. Once you're ready to create your own layout, select Start A new Plan from the main menu.

If you do not have a CD-ROM drive, download *HomePlan* from either America Online and CompuServe. On America Online, locate the file HOME27.EXE (120,852 bytes) by searching the software libraries. On CompuServe, look for HomePlan in the Zenith Forum, Library 6, under the name HOMEPN.ZIP, or in the Dwellings forum, Library 16, under the name HOMEPL.ZIP. You can also order the commercial version of the program, Homeplan Pro. HomePlan Pro provides a graphical, Windows-type interface, additional symbol libraries, and many other features.

Design-A-Room is a Windows shareware layout program. A copy of it is also on the CD included with this book. The shareware version lets you create rooms up to 40-by-25 feet, and you can put rooms together on the same page for a complete floor plan. The program includes 17 symbols for walls, doors, and fixtures, as well as 31 furniture symbols for couches, pianos, tables, pool table, fireplaces, and more. You can turn off and on its snap-to-grid feature to position symbols.

As you position walls and symbols, their precise position and size appear on the status line. You can also position objects by referencing horizontal and vertical scale lines.

The registered version of the program allows you to create larger rooms, and it includes an "Add Text" option to place text anywhere on the screen—even on top of other icons.

To learn more about the program after you've downloaded it from the CD, select Contents from the Help menu. You can also read the file DESIGN.WRI. The document will be in the directory where you selected to install the program.

If you do not have a CD-ROM drive, download Design-A-Room from Compu-Serve's Winshare forum—look in library 10 for the file DES23.ZIP (184,539 bytes).

So how do you select a layout program that's just right for you? If you want 3D images with substantial layout capabilities, choose either FloorPlan Plus 3D or 3D Home Architect. If three-dimensional images are not important, then consider Key Home CAD, Design Your Own Home Architecture, or Planix Home—listed here from the least to the most sophisticated and detailed.

Features of Commercial Layout Programs

Layout Program	Vendor	Features
FloorPlan Plus 3D	Computer Easy (800) 522-3279	Detailed symbol customizing; 13 pre-defined layers and 20 floors; roof editor; 3D wireframe and solid views; auto wall alignment and dimension lines

Features of Commercial Layout Programs (Continued)

Layout Program	Vendor	Features
3D Home Architect	Broderbund Software, Inc. (800) 521-6263	Auto wall alignment and external dimension lines; reverse plan; plan check; building material reports; elevation, overview, and camera views; four floors and foundation layers; CD with multimedia tips
Autodesk Home	Autodesk (707) 794-1450	DOS interface; floor, roof, and siding fill options; symbols in plan and elevation views; prints shopping list; compatible with Kitchen and Bath for room details
Key Home CAD	Softkey (407) 367-0005	Six user-defined layers
Key Home Designer CD	Softkey (407) 367-0005	User-definable symbol libraries
Design Your Own Home Architecture	Abracadata Ltd (800) 541-4871	Nine layers and composite base layer; many symbols in elevation view; stud tool; building materials lists; compatible with Design Your Own Home Interiors
Planix Home	Foresight Resources Corporation (800) 231-8574	Shell dialog box for overall shape; extensive symbol libraries; 22 predefined layers; 14 reports; 500-floor-plan CD; symbol editor; complete printed catalog of symbols

Inspecting Your Home

Whether you are having an addition built, remodeling a room, or building a new house, you should inspect the work completely before paying the contractor.

If you are new to looking at houses, get some advice on the inspection process. Use *Home Inspector,* on the CD accompanying this book, to learn how to inspect your home improvement project before paying the contractor. This DOS program gives you a point-by-point checklist of the major systems to inspect.

Major Systems Covered in the Home Inspector

✔ Electrical

✔ Plumbing

✔ Heating and cooling

✔ Kitchens

✔ Baths

✔ Other rooms

✔ Attic

✔ Doors and windows

✔ Roof

From the main menu, select Inspection Checklist to learn what to look for during the inspection. You can also select Inspection Hints to learn some of the tricks of the trade, or select Diagrams to see graphics explaining heating, draining, and hot water systems.

The CD also includes a demonstration of a commercial version of Home Inspector for Windows. Pull down selections from the program's menu bar to see the inspection details covered by the program. While some of the options will be dimmed and unselectactable for this demo version, you can choose at least one option from each menu. Use the PREV, NEXT, MAIN MENU, and TIPS buttons that appear on the bottom of the screen to navigate through the program. If clicking on the PREV or NEXT buttons has no effect, return to the main menu.

➡ *The Case of the Amateur Architects*

Nancy and Stephen were trying to build a new home on a rather tight budget. So before hiring an architect, they consulted with local authorities about building codes, land use requirements, and possible setbacks. After determining the maximum size of the house that could fit on their lot, they purchased several home plan books and selected a design that fit their needs and lifestyle. The layout, however, lacked a few essential elements. Nancy purchased a CAD program and reconstructed the layout on her computer. Nancy and Stephen then modified the design by moving walls and enlarging a bath and the kitchen. Using their modified layout and the original plans as a base, they saved quite a bit on architect's fees.

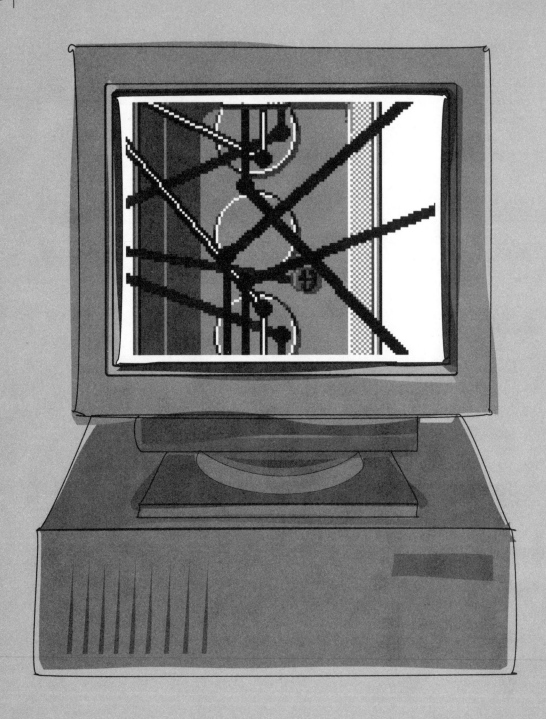

4

Getting How-To Help

Fireplaces & Wood Stoves

Insulation & Weather Stripping

Roofs

Walls

Now

that you've planned and budgeted for your home improvement project, you are ready to complete it. You can per-
form many household repairs and improvements yourself, even if you are not
completely experienced at it. Using your computer, you can learn

➡ How to make a repair or improvement

➡ Which tools you'll need and how to use them

➡ Professional tricks of the trade

Do It Yourself

Using your computer, you can get step-by-step instructions and learn how to
use tools. Multimedia programs will illustrate how to make repairs, how to install fixtures and appliances, and even how to complete additions and major
improvements.

Before you start a home improvement project, however, you must first make
the do-it-yourself decision. Should you do the project yourself, or should you
hire a contractor to do it for you?

If you are an experienced do-it-yourselfer, or are just handy with tools, then
you *can* perform many home repair and improvement projects yourself. However, if you are at all unsure of your skills, then take some time to decide the
best course of action. First, ask yourself these questions:

➡ Have I performed a similar project before?

➡ Have I used the tools and materials before?

If you answered Yes to either or both of these questions, then you can probably complete the project yourself—**even if do need a little more how-to help
and information.**

But don't give up hope if you answered No to the questions. Take a second
test using your experience in planning the project, as you learned to do in
Chapter 2:

➡ Will I be able to plan the project without difficulty?

➡ Do I understand all of the terminology involved?

➔ Can I estimate the materials I'll need?

➔ Do I have the tools to perform the project?

➔ Do I have the time to complete the project?

If you answered No to any of these questions, then consider hiring a contractor. Of course, hiring the right contractor for the job also requires planning and skill. For help in making that decision, download these files from CompuServe:

➔ Mary Gilliatt's Tips On Hiring Professionals, the file MGSHGS.TXT from the Dwellings Forum.

➔ Select a Remodeling Contractor, the file PDRMCN.TXT also in the Dwellings Forum.

➔ Find The Right Person To Work On Your Home, the file HIRING.TXT, from the Family Handyman Forum.

If you answered Yes to either set of questions, then you are a good candidate for undertaking a do-it-yourself project. But before starting the project, use your computer to get how-to information.

Getting How-To Help Online

If you subscribe to an online service or have access to shareware collections, then there are literally thousands of programs and files available to you. Online services are an excellent source of information on home maintenance and repair.

On America Online, get how-to information from the Homeowners Forum and from HOME Magazine Online. In the Homeowners Forum, select the Home Improvement option, and then pick Repair & Maintenance from the menu. You can then access informative articles and tips from professionals. Read an article online or use the File, Save As command to download the article to your hard disk.

In the HOME Magazine Online area, select Interactive Home and then go to the Project Management Center, where you'll find a series of message boards. Select Remodeling and Renovating to access a message board for posting questions and for sharing your knowledge.

To download software from America Online, pull down the Go To menu and select Search Software Libraries. Enter a keyword or phase that you want to search for, and then click on the button labeled List Matching Files. For example, use keywords such as home *repair*, home improvement, and remodeling.

On America Online, get how-to information from the Homeowners Forum and from HOME Magazine Online

You'll find a number of useful programs and text files, such as Hints & Tips, from Joy's Software. Hints & Tips is a useful shareware program that contains tips and suggestions on a wide range of household projects and problems. You'll find this program on the CD included with this book. You can select one of the options from a menu that appears when you run the program to see detailed information on a variety of subjects. For example, select the Handyman option for using tools and performing repairs. You can also download the program from America Online as the file HINTS.ZIP (47,740 bytes).

~ 🖥 ~

CompuServe offers two sources of how-to information: the Dwellings Forum and the Family Handyman Forum.

The Dwellings Forum contains hundreds of how-to files and messages. Browse the libraries and message boards to find the information you need to complete a project, or for general reference. You'll find specific how-to help in the Repairs/Remodeling section. For instance, Red's Home Maintenance Program contains 21 categories of information for the do-it-yourselfer, from Appliances to Windows. Download the program as POTEET.ZIP (122,250 bytes).

CompuServe's Family Handyman Forum, presented by Family Handyman Magazine, is another excellent source of how-to help. As with all CompuServe Forums, it includes a library section for sharing programs and files and a message area for communicating with other Forum members. Library sections are devoted to the areas shown here.

Use the Forum for general information, such as downloading Home Repair Special, a text file explaining how to correct common household problems.

How-to sections of CompuServe's Family Handyman Forum

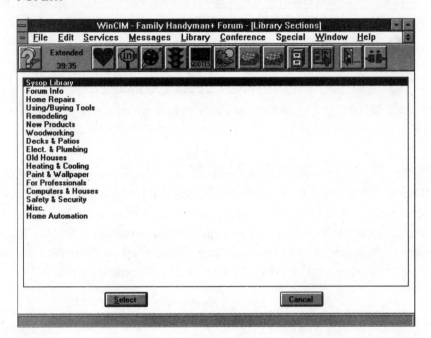

You'll find the file under HMREPR.TXT (18,048 bytes). You can also get step-by-step help for specific problems and projects. Here's just a sample of the resources:

- WINDOW.TXT (16,609 bytes) presents step-by-step instructions for replacing a window.

- CRWNML.TXT (15,069 bytes) gives instructions for installing crown molding.

- FASTEN.ZIP (1,079,808 bytes) explains how to remove stubborn screws and nails.

- FURRP.ZIP (1,441,792 bytes) shows how to repair furniture.

- REGLAZ.ZIP (4,566 bytes) gives step-by-step instructions on how to resurface a bathtub.

Some files from this Forum require a special viewer program to display on your screen. You download the viewer from the Forum's Library 0.

The Forum also contains text files explaining how to select and use tools, such as the following:

➜ RADSAW.TXT (5,676 bytes) explains how to use a radial arm saw.

➜ CLAMPS.TXT (4,131 bytes) tells how to choose and use clamps.

➜ ROUTER.TXT (5,796 bytes) is a guide to using a router.

➜ MITER.TXT (3,948 bytes) explains how to use a power miter box.

If you are on the Internet, get in touch with the misc.consumers.house Usenet group. You'll find useful information and lively discussions, as well as Frequently Asked Questions (FAQs) on a number of issues. When you access the group you'll see a listing of message threads. A *message thread* is a topic about which one or more messages have been posted on the system.

For example, you may see a listing that contains these entries:

```
Upgrading Wiring in Old House (5 msgs)
Basement Ventilation
Installing Window Trim (3 msgs)
```

This means that five messages have been posted regarding upgrading household wiring, one message on basement ventilation, and three messages about window trim.

Use the facilities of your system to read or download messages, to create your own topic, or to reply to a question or comment in a current thread.

Through the Internet you can also access the HouseNet BBS. This bulletin board is sponsored by Owens-Corning and operated by Gene and Katie Hamilton. Reach the service via telnet at the address Housenet.com. Telnet is an Internet service that lets you log on to a remote computer network. You can also dial directly into the BBS via modem at (410) 745-2037. The service offers message boards, chat lines, and a software library—all devoted to home improvement. The over 150,000 messages probably contain answers to most of your how-to questions. Future plans for the board include a database of tips and materials estimators.

Learning about Tools and How to Use Them

For more comprehensive information on repair and maintenance, consider three multimedia programs on CD-ROM. You'll get expert advice and step-by-step directions for using tools and performing many home improvement jobs.

Hometime Weekend Home Projects, from IVI Publishing, is based on the popular Hometime series on public television. It is organized into twelve areas:

- Ceramic tile
- Plumbing
- Framing
- Hand and power tools
- Windows, doors, and trim
- Wiring and lighting
- Cabinets and counters
- Wallpaper
- Flooring
- Paints and stains
- Drywall
- Building a deck

Each area offers a series of video clips explaining methods of installation and maintenance. You can also choose to display materials, tips, and tools. Many areas have utilities, such as a materials calculator, shopping list, or a list of suppliers and other resources for additional information. For example, the drywall calculator lets you enter the height of the room and the total measurement of the perimeter. It then calculates the materials needed and displays the shopping list. To get the most from this program, you will need a sound card and a double-speed CD-ROM drive.

Simply House, from 4Home Productions, offers you several ways to find home-related information. You can click on a room or section of a blueprint to see related topics. You can also select from a series of 25 category buttons, from Attics to Walls.

> **Use a CD-ROM guide such as Simply House for multimedia how-to information**

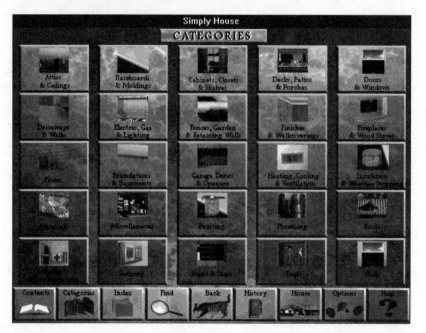

The over 500 pages of text and advice are from the *Stanley Complete Step-by-Step Book of Home Repair and Improvement*. There are more than 1,400 full-color illustrations and 100 animations. Most topics offer information on installation, repair, maintenance, design, and saving time and money. You get step-by-step advice, with informative graphics and an easy-to-use interface with buttons leading to specific information and related topics.

Also consider *The Home Repair Encyclopedia*, from Books That Work. This CD is organized into 11 chapters:

- ➡ Emergencies
- ➡ Tools
- ➡ Plumbing

- Electrical
- Heating and cooling
- Floors and walls
- Painting
- Outdoors
- Roofs and basements
- Rental tools
- Working with pros

Information is provided in text, sound, and animation formats. Each screen has buttons you can use to access additional information relating to older houses, money-saving tips, tools, and safety.

The encyclopedia also includes four survival guides that provide detailed information on adhesives, paints, stain removal, and toll-free telephone numbers. Each guide presents an easy-to-use dialog box. For example, in the adhesive guide, you select the materials you want to bond together, you specify the setting speed, and you indicate whether or not the bond must be waterproof. The guide then recommends the type of adhesive.

The paint guide is similar. You select either interior or exterior application, the type of material and object being painted, and some desired specifications. The guide then recommends a type of paint.

There are also three estimators included in The Home Repair Encyclopedia:

- The attic venting estimator calculates the free vent area required for adequate attic ventilation.
- The concrete estimator calculates the amount of concrete required to fill an area.
- The paint estimator calculates the number of gallons of paint needed for a room.

If you do not have a CD-ROM drive, Books That Work markets a number of programs on floppy disk, including a version of the encyclopedia called *The Home Survival Toolkit*. The toolkit includes many of the same features that the CD version has, including multimedia presentations.

These general how-to guides are excellent resources. However, you may want some additional help when making electrical or plumbing repairs.

Making Electrical Repairs

Performing electrical repairs without adequate knowledge can be dangerous, both to you and your house. If you know what you're doing, however, you can save money by making repairs and improvements yourself, rather than hiring an electrician. Before actually connecting wires, however, you may want to get how-to information using your computer.

Get Wired!, from Books That Work, explains the basics of home electricity, how to do your own repairs, and how to add new wiring. There is also a section on wiring your home for the "information highway," including details of installing home video, coaxial cables, and telephone equipment.

Even though the program comes on floppy disks instead of a CD, many subjects use multimedia to show you how to perform the repair. For example, if you need to install a remodel box for a new outlet, run the animation to see and hear each step explained.

The program includes the same electrical estimators found in the Home Repair Encyclopedia, as well as sections on troubleshooting fluorescent lights and short circuits. The Hardware Store Survival Guide shows pictures of electrical items you'll need to purchase for your project, along with their names, nicknames, and descriptions.

Icons on the screen quickly lead you to additional information. Clicking on the Old House icon, for example, gives information relating to wiring older houses. The Safety icon has warnings to help you avoid injury.

One of the most entertaining and educational sections of Get Wired! is the Circuit Simulator. The simulator includes 24 interactive wiring diagrams that you can examine and modify. You can also create your own diagrams to match your project. Add switches, lights, and other loads to the circuit, connect the wires, and even add plastic connectors just as you would in real life.

Create your circuit in the simulator before you actually wire a home improvement project. The program sends "virtual" electricity through the circuit, warning you of code violations and potential problems. Once you design the correct circuit, print out a copy of the diagram to use as a guide for the actual wiring.

➔ ### The Get Wired! Circuit Simulator

Print out a copy of the correct virtual circuit to use as a guide in the real world.

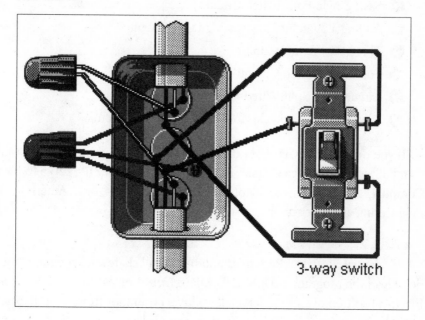

3-way switch

You can purchase the simulator separately from Books that Work as the Wiring Circuit Planner and Simulator, one in the Home Project Series.

There are also a number of excellent shareware guides for the do-it-yourself electrician. The program Your Electrical Reference Source, for example, is on the CD included with this book.

Because the program is written as a Windows help file, you can use the familiar techniques to move from subject to subject. There is a contents page listing its major topics, a search function for finding specific information, and jump terms to quickly move from subject to subject.

While not every feature of the program is available in the shareware version, enough are accessible to make it a useful reference. For example, a section entitled "Common Errors By The DIYer" serves as a quick reference on how to avoid typical wiring problems. There is also information on residential circuit requirements, wiring methods, and tips. A section on specific circuits illustrates and explains how to wire these common jobs:

- ➡ Basic Single Pole Switch Circuit
- ➡ Adding a Switch to an Existing Light/Circuit
- ➡ Three-Way Switch Circuit
- ➡ Four-Way Switch Circuit
- ➡ Circuit for a Split Wired Receptacle
- ➡ Switch and Receptacle Combination Device Circuit

If you do not have CD-ROM drive, you can download the program from CompuServe or America Online. Look for the file SASW.ZIP (220,546 bytes) in CompuServe's Dwellings and Home Handyman Forums, or in America Online's Engineering and Science library section.

~🖥~

Residential Electrical Reports is another useful shareware program. You can download the program as DEMAND.ZIP (342,144 bytes) from the Plumbing\Electrical section of CompuServe's Dwellings Forum, or from the Database Support library on America Online. This program calculates service requirements for new or existing homes. If you are planning an addition or major upgrade, the program will help determine if your current electrical service is adequate. Professional electricians can use this program as well.

The program takes you step-by-step through a series of questions to determine every electrical load. It then calculates the total demand in watts and the minimum service size in amps.

~🖥~

The Dwellings and Family Handyman Forums on CompuServe offer a variety of how-to files for electrical repair. On the Family Handyman Forum, look for these files:

- OUTLET.TXT (6,985 bytes) explains how to install a junction box in walls.
- ELCTRC.TXT (13,217 bytes) presents Dos and Don'ts of electrical repair
- ELEC.TXT (14,001 bytes) lists common wiring mistakes by do-it-yourselfers

The CD packaged with this book includes two graphics files—SINGLE.BMP and THREEWAY.BMP—that show how to wire a single pole switch and a three-way switch. The files are in BMP (bitmap) format, which you can open in Paintbrush.

If you are planning a project that includes an electrical appliance, you may want to calculate how much it will cost to run that appliance. Look on the appliance's faceplate for its rating in amps and volts. You'll also need to estimate how many hours the appliance runs each day and the cost of a kilowatt hour of electricity in your area. You can find the kilowatt charges on your electric bill.

To make the calculation, multiply the rating of the appliance in amps by its voltage. Multiply that result by the number of hours each day the appliance is used, and then multiply that result by 365. This gives you the number of watts used by the appliance each year. Divide the number of watts by 1,000 to compute kilowatt hours. Finally, multiply the kilowatt hours by the cost of each kilowatt in your area.

A worksheet to perform these calculations is provided on the CD included with this book. The worksheet is called ELECEST.XLS if you use Microsoft Excel, and ELECEST.WKS if you use Lotus 1-2-3.

Plumbing How-To

Many homeowners are hesitant to make plumbing repairs for fear of causing a flood. It is certainly more difficult to work with pipes and water pressure than it is to work with wiring. However, you can perform many plumbing repairs and installations using basic tools and a little know-how.

➡ Track your appliance expenses.

Use a spreadsheet like the one shown here to calculate the cost of running an appliance.

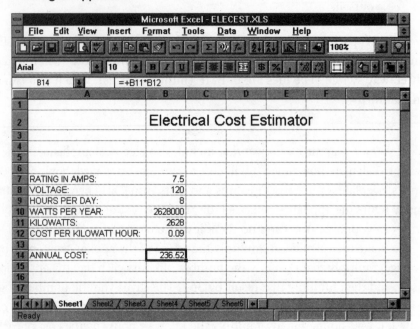

Again, here is where your computer can help. You can find how-to information online from most services, such as CompuServe and the HouseNet BBS.

On CompuServe's Home Handyman Forum, for example, scan through library 8 for shareware software and text files explaining plumbing repairs. Some files to look for include

- ➡ DRAIN.TXT (2,378 bytes) is a guide to unclogging drains.
- ➡ FAUCET.TXT (7,833 bytes) explains how to repair dripping faucets.
- ➡ COPPIP.ZIP (711,177 bytes) describes how to sweat copper tubing, and comes complete with color photos.
- ➡ TOILET.TXT (7,929 bytes) explains how to repair a toilet.
- ➡ PLUMB.TXT (13,373 bytes) shows you to join pipes of all types.

In the Dwellings Forum, browse through library 7. You'll find information on sweating copper pipes and repairing Kohler faucets.

For a more comprehensive guide to plumbing, consider *Plumbing: Essential Repairs*, a multimedia guide from Books That Work. *Plumbing: Essential Repairs* is supplied on floppy disks, so you don't need a CD-ROM drive. This program provides detailed information on troubleshooting and repairing plumbing problems, with special tips from the pros. Before attempting to repair a faucet, you can view the multimedia presentation and then print out the step-by-step guide.

The program's Hardware Survival Guide illustrates all of the tools and supplies you'll need to make plumbing repairs. Review this section before visiting your local hardware store. Make sure you have the proper tools, and that you know exactly what supplies to purchase to complete the project.

➔ The Case of the Consummate Consumer

Miriam, a new homeowner, was just learning how to use tools and make repairs. So when she decided to add a porch to her house, she also decided to hire a contractor. Because she had heard horror stories about scams and ripoffs, Miriam consulted her local Better Business Bureau, and she also went online with CompuServe. In the Dwellings Forum she found two text files that really gave her an education—Contract Basics for Remodeling and Building (TOHCON.TXT) and Glossary of Terms Used by Builders and Remodelers (JCGLOS.TXT). Armed with the knowledge she gained from these sources, she felt confident interviewing contractors. Her new porch is now a treasured part of her family's house.

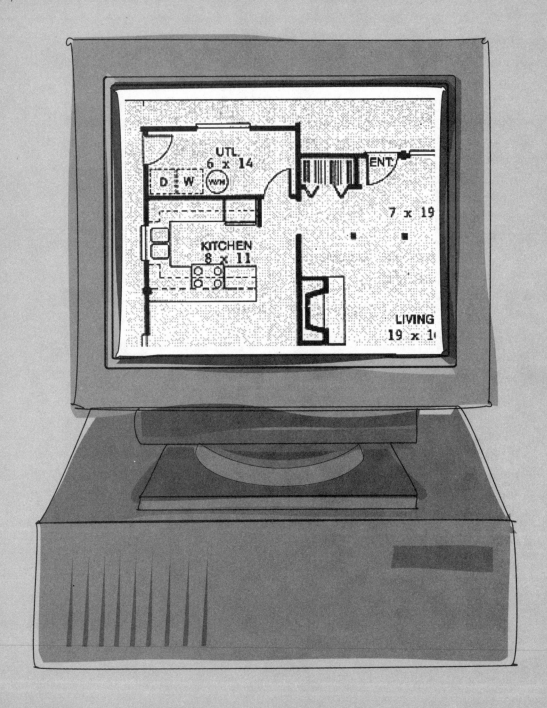

5 | *Planning* Kitchens *and* Baths

Of all the rooms in your house, your kitchen and bathrooms can be the most expensive. The cost of fixtures, appliances, and cabinets—and the labor to install them—quickly accumulates. Both of these rooms are also often difficult to lay out because they are relatively small and they need access to water, electricity, and other utilities.

Fortunately, your computer can help. You can get expert advice on room design and even "see" your rooms before you spend the time and expense to complete them.

Before planning your rooms, you should learn the basic principles of kitchen and bath layout. You can get this information from computer software or from online resources, such as forums and bulletin boards.

Learning about Room Design Online

America Online, CompuServe, and other services contain a wealth of practical information, graphics files, and the experiences of other homeowners who have designed their own kitchens and baths.

➲ Online home design resources

These online services provide excellent resources to help you plan the interior of your home.

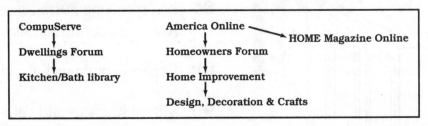

On CompuServe, get information from the Dwellings Forum. In the Kitchens/Baths library section, for example, you'll find text files explaining kitchen design, layout, and construction. You'll find these two excerpts from *This Old House*

Kitchens and *This Old House Bathrooms*, books from Steve Thomas and Philip Langdon of the popular television series on PBS:

➜ TOHWT.TXT—How to design your kitchen work area

➜ TOHDP.TXT—Early steps in designing a kitchen

The Dwellings Forum also has excerpts from other popular books and information from designers and contractors.

The Kitchen/Baths message section contains lively and informative conversations, questions, and answers about kitchen and bath design.

CompuServe's Home Handyman Forum is largely devoted to how-to information. However, you will also find the file BATHRO.ZIP, a collection of 12 complete bathroom designs, from a basic powder room to a master bath complete with a whirlpool tub and walk-in closets.

If you subscribe to America Online, go to the Homeowner's Forum. To view or download articles on room and house design, select the Home Improvement button and then choose Design & Decoration. Check out the forum's message boards—look in the Design, Decoration & Crafts section for questions and answers about kitchen and bath design. Also go to America Online's HOME Magazine section. You'll find interesting articles in the forum's main menu, as well as information in the message center and the manufacturers information center. You can also search back issues of *HOME Magazine* for articles and design tips.

Multimedia Kitchens and Baths

For multimedia information on room design, there's a wide variety of CD-ROM products to choose from. The CD version of 3D Home Architect, for example, includes sections devoted to kitchens, baths, and cabinets. In Home Pro video clips, Gerry Connell shows you the basics of design and material selection, supplementing the text that appears on screen.

The Kitchen section of the program contains these four categories: Design, Appliances, Counters, and Sinks.

Complete House

Use a multimedia program, such as Complete House (shown here) to learn about kitchen and bath design.

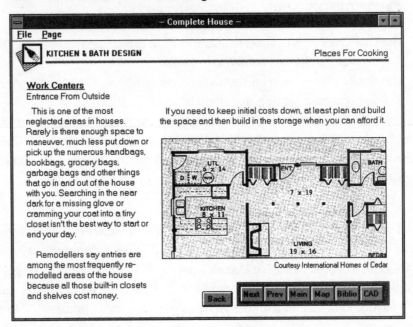

The Design category explains the basics of kitchen layout and space planning, shows how to design a safe kitchen, and gives recommendations from the National Kitchen and Bath Association. The other categories explain about materials, design, and the selection of appliances, sinks, and counters. You'll be amazed by the variety of options available to you.

The Bath section focuses on these areas of bath design:

- Fixtures
- Lighting, venting, and heat
- Safety
- Space
- Storage and counters

Though bathrooms are usually the smallest rooms of your house, a lot of planning must go into their design. Proper layout is necessary to take advantage of limited space while making the room convenient and easy to use.

Good cabinet placement and design are essential to both kitchens and baths. The cabinet section of 3D Home Architect discusses these areas:

- Cabinetry and storage
- Stock, semicustom, and custom cabinets
- Material and finish
- Frame versus frameless construction
- Construction terms
- Door options
- Storage options
- Checklist of materials

You can also learn about design from the Kitchen and Bath section of Key Home Designer and Complete House. The programs do not use animations, but they include high-quality photographs and audio clips.

Both programs present kitchen information in five categories:

- *First Steps in Kitchen Design* shows you how to prepare for planning a kitchen.
- *Work Centers* illustrates the historical development of the kitchen, and it shows you fundamental kitchen arrangements.
- *Workflows and Areas* shows you how to lay out a kitchen for maximum efficiency and usefulness.
- *Sample Kitchen Layouts* displays photographs and illustrated floor plans of basic kitchen layouts.
- *Prize Winners* displays photographs of award-winning kitchens.

You'll learn about the history of kitchens, and you'll learn the importance of kitchen location, entrances, traffic patterns, and space allotment. Sample designs thoroughly explain basic kitchen layouts, such as galley, L-shaped, U-shaped, island, and peninsula. The program includes similar categories for bathrooms.

Planning—A Step-by-Step Guide

Bathrooms and kitchens reflect more about you and your lifestyle than any other room of your house. Before actually designing these rooms, carefully consider their content and use.

With your kitchen, start the design process by evaluating the kitchen you have right now. First, make a simple count of the number of drawers and cabinets. Do you need more? Could you do with any less?

Now use a program such as Paintbrush to create a simple layout of your cabinets and drawers. It doesn't have to be fancy. Mark down what you store in the cabinets and drawers so you can see how you use your current space. Print out a copy of the drawing and save it on your disk.

Next, draw a basic floor plan showing the position of your major appliances, counter space, and cabinets. You don't need to use a layout program at this stage—a quick sketch using Paintbrush will do just as well. Draw lines on the basic floor plan showing the flow of objects from cabinet to appliance—such as taking a pot from the cabinet and placing it on the stove, or carrying a glass to the sink for a drink of water, or moving a utensil to your food preparation area. Make a note if the current arrangement is inconvenient, or if you could improve on the work flow.

In kitchens, pay particular attention to work flow using your Paintbrush drawings. You'll find that the most common traffic pattern is a triangle between the sink, range, and refrigerator. Avoid placing a major appliance so the work flow passes through the triangle. You also need to keep a comfortable distance between the points of the triangle. Placing the points too far apart will make them inconvenient; placing them too close will give the kitchen a cramped appearance. Many designers recommend that the total distance around the triangle be between 12 and 21 feet.

The path to designing an efficient kitchen

Use a simple draw or paint program such as Paintbrush to draw a floor plan of your kitchen and its work flow.

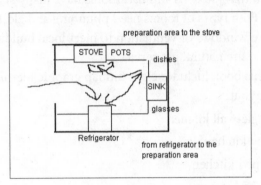

Make a note of what contents have special requirements. For example, do your pots require extra height or width? Do small appliances, such as a blender or food processor, require extra space?

Finally, measure the size of appliances such as the sink, stove, and refrigerator. Mark the sizes on the drawing, and then consider if you need larger appliances, or smaller ones, in your dream kitchen. Measure the height of the counter top from the floor. While 36 inches is the standard height used in most kitchen construction, taller members of your family might be more comfortable with a higher countertop, for example, or shorter members might prefer a shorter countertop.

You can do the same sort of planning with a bathroom. Make a sketch showing the size and position of bathroom fixtures, vanities, and other cabinets. Note if you need a higher or lower sink height, more space between fixtures, or other special needs, such as handrails.

Design Considerations

Once you are familiar with kitchen and bath design and know what you need in these rooms, you can work with your architect or contractor to create the perfect rooms for your house. Use your Paintbrush drawings to help explain the type of kitchen and baths you want.

You can also lay out the rooms yourself. Before drawing walls and adding fixtures, however, keep in mind that kitchens and bathrooms have many special requirements and limitations. Both types of rooms need plumbing and electrical service, and they may require windows or ventilation to meet local building codes. A kitchen may also require natural gas service.

The CD packaged with this book includes eight bitmap graphic files illustrating basic kitchen and bath layout:

- WALLKIT.BMP, a single-wall kitchen
- GALLEY.BMP, a galley kitchen
- L-KIT.BMP, an L-shaped kitchen
- U-KIT.BMP, a U-shaped kitchen
- WALLBATH.BMP, a single-wall bathroom
- GALLEYB.BMP, a galley bathroom
- L-BATH.BMP, an L-shaped bathroom
- U-BATH.BMP, a U-shaped bathroom

You can open these bitmap files in Windows Paintbrush. Experiment with the kitchen designs by visualizing how you would go about preparing a meal, moving around the kitchen between appliances and counters.

Incorporating Furnishings and Accommodating Families

The sketches you make during the planning stages will help you make some basic decisions about your kitchen or bath. Before you start tearing down walls and spending money, however, you should create a detailed layout. You'll want to lay out the design to scale so you can easily make precise measurements and order the correct cabinets, appliances, and fixtures. You can also use a detailed layout to plan the exact placement of appliances and fixtures.

If you want to see an example of how the design process transforms an old kitchen into a new one, look in the Repairs/Remodeling section of CompuServe's Dwellings Forum. You'll find a series of graphics files illustrating a complete kitchen remodeling project from Don Arnoldy:

- MYKIT1.GIF—the original floorplan
- MYKIT2.GIF—perspective drawing of the floorplan
- MYKIT3.GIF—perspective view of proposed kitchen
- MYKIT4.GIF—floor plans for proposed kitchen

All of the layout programs described in Chapter 3 can be used to design the details of kitchens and baths. They all include symbols for fixtures, appliances, cabinets, and furniture. Some also provide electrical and plumbing objects that you'll need for detailed blueprints.

Your software decision should be based on your personal needs and skills. An architect or contractor, for example, may prefer a layout program with precise CAD and measurement capabilities. They look at the design from a very practical point of view so they can determine the placement of every stud, wire, wall, and pipe.

A kitchen and bath designer, on the other hand, looks at the layout in terms of convenience, utility, and the quality of the living space. That is exactly the way you should look at kitchen and bath design. A kitchen and bath should accommodate, not dictate, your lifestyle. It should be designed to incorporate the furnishings that make you comfortable. It should flow naturally with your everyday activities.

For this reason, programs that display three-dimensional or side views are best suited for the task. Three-dimensional programs let you better experience the environment, rather than attempt to picture it from a two-dimensional plan.

Programs that provide three-dimensional and side views also typically let you experiment with color and the texture of surfaces. Not only can you get a feel for the flow of the space, you can experience the look and the atmosphere. They allow you to change the color of walls, floors, cabinets, and appliances to select a color scheme that you'll be able to live with into the future.

Experimenting with Layouts

There are several programs designed specially to lay out the interior of your house. These may lack some of the features of other layout programs, but they include a greater variety of interior symbols. We will look at two such programs, one for Windows and one for DOS. Both provide CAD-like capabilities, three-dimensional or side views, and the ability to experiment with color.

Design Your Own Home Interiors, available from Abracadata, offers the same easy-to-use interface as Design Your Own Home Architecture, but without layers. It contains 12 symbol libraries devoted to interior design:

- Appliances
- Bathroom
- Bedroom
- Dining room
- Doors
- Electronics
- Kitchens
- Lights
- Living rooms
- Miscellaneous
- Office
- Windows

While the program is not advertised as three-dimensional, it does offer three-dimensional side views. In side view, the program converts the two-dimensional objects to 3-D, so you can picture yourself standing at each end of the room looking toward the far wall. While you cannot "walk around" the room as you can with three-dimensional layout programs, you can just click on an icon to change positions from one wall to another.

See your kitchen from the side.

Side views of Design Your Own Home Interiors show a three-dimensional image of your room.

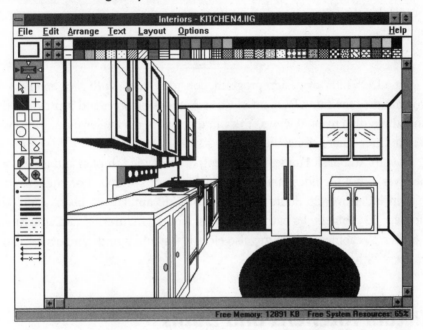

As with Design Your Own Home Architecture, you can create your own symbols. If you want to see your symbol in three-dimensional side view, however, you must create each of these views yourself:

- Top
- Left
- Right
- Front
- Back
- First quarter
- Second quarter
- Third quarter

➜ Fourth quarter

You use the program's drawing tools to create sketches of the object in these views. You then assign each of the sketches to one of the views. When you display the layout in side view, the program uses the sketch appropriate to the perspective.

For a DOS interior design program, consider *Autodesk Kitchen and Bath*. This program uses the same DOS interface as Autodesk Home, and it provides the same three-dimensional views. You can display rooms in elevation, birdseye, and two- or three-dimensional view.

As with Autodesk Home, the symbols are provided in plan and elevation perspectives, but it includes many additional interior symbols. For kitchens, the program includes over 25 doors and 6 windows, 13 appliances, 8 sinks and faucets, and over 50 cabinets. Its bath symbols include 18 fixtures, 4 medicine cabinets, and over 25 cabinets. There are also electrical symbols and symbols for handrails for users with special needs.

Virtual Kitchens and Baths

If you want a real virtual reality design experience, consider *3D Virtual Reality Room Planner*. It is not a true CAD program because it lacks the details you'd need to prepare blueprint-quality designs, such as layers, stairs, and electrical symbols.

As with other layout programs, you create a floor plan, and you position basic pieces of furniture, appliances, and fixtures. The program supplies only one window type, although you can change its height and width and its distance from the floor. You can select from eight door styles, and you can flip a door to change its opening direction.

Basic symbols included with the program are organized by room:

➜ Den

➜ Patio

➡ Office

➡ Living room

➡ Bedroom

➡ Dining room

➡ Kitchen

➡ Bathroom

There aren't a lot of symbols in each category, but there are enough to get the overall layout of a room. The only symbol that you can create yourself is a generic box.

What places this program into its own category, however, is its virtual reality walk-though, a true real-time experience. Two-dimensional walls and objects are converted and displayed in three dimensions. You use the mouse or keyboard to "walk through" the layout from room to room. There is no delay as you move around the three-dimensional cyberspace, although it takes some practice to avoid walking through walls and windows. A menu even lets you adjust the ambient light to simulate various lighting conditions.

You probably wouldn't choose 3D Virtual Reality Room Planner if you were building a house or creating blueprints. However, its virtual walk-through is certainly fun. It is an excellent way to visualize the actual flow and layout of a room, to experience living in it without the long delays experienced when moving around in other three-dimensional programs.

Selecting Fixtures and Appliances

You can control the cost of a major kitchen or bath renovation by making wise buying decisions. If you are hiring a contractor to remodel, get several estimates, as explained in Chapter 2. If you are performing the work yourself, then you'll need to do some detailed planning.

Because of the expense of cabinets, fixtures, and appliances, you should select these items carefully. While price will be a major determining factor, remember that you may be living with your new kitchen and bath for a long time, so don't skimp on the important stuff.

Use a spreadsheet to plan your overall remodeling budget. Start by entering the total amount you'd like to spend, and then list each of the expenses, including labor costs. Next, create a cell to represent the amount remaining. In the worksheet shown here, which is included as KITCHEN.XLS and KITCHEN.WKS on the CD accompanying this book, cell D2 represents the available funds.

As you price items, enter the expenses in cells D4 through D25. Cell G2 calculates the remaining funds using the formula +D2-SUM(D4:D25). As you enter costs, watch the remaining amount to see how far your budget can stretch.

➡ Create a worksheet to track your expenses and budget.

	Microsoft Excel - KITCHEN.XLS								
File	**Edit**	**View**	**Insert**	**Format**	**Tools**	**Data**	**Window**	**Help**	

G2   =+D2-SUM(D4:D25)

	A	B	C	D	E	F	G	H	I	J
1										
2			Proposed Budget:	10000		Remaining:	1420			
3										
4	Expenses		Cabinets	3200						
5			Labor	1000						
6			Counters	500						
7			Labor	250						
8			Plumbing	215						
9			Floor	250						
10			Labor							
11			Lights	125						
12			Labor							
13			Oven	900						
14			Refrigerator	1250						
15			Dishwasher	325						
16			Furniture	565						
17		Other:								
18										

Sheet1 / Sheet2 / Sheet3 / Sheet4 / Sheet5 / Sheet6

Ready

With your budget planned, its time to comparison shop. Record the specifications of every cabinet, appliance, and fixture that you'll need to purchase; then go to several showrooms, look through catalogs, or visit your local building supply or home center. As you shop, make certain the items you consider meet the specifications, and record any installation or delivery costs. Don't be beguiled by trendy items with extra features that will drive your costs above budget.

In shopping for items, also consider the utility requirements of kitchen appliances. For example, a commercial electric stove that requires 200 volts or a high-amp circuit may cost you additional electrician's fees. You also need to consider the appliance's size and weight. Large commercial appliances and luxurious hot tubs require a strong floor.

If you find that prices are generally higher than you imagined, then go back and reconsider your budget and the details of the project. Make adjustments where possible. Switch to a less expensive floor, countertop, or appliance, for example. You might also decide to refinish or reface your existing cabinets rather than replace them.

To renovate your kitchen on budget, look for these files in the Dwellings Forum of CompuServe:

- ➡ MGSHKD.TXT—practical and economical kitchen ideas
- ➡ MGSHCB.TXT—kitchen cabinets on a budget
- ➡ LLWDOC.TXT—quick face lifts for kitchen cabinets

Programs You Can Use to Redesign Your Home

Program	Manufacturer	Platform	Key Features
Design Your Own Home Interiors	Abracadata Ltd. (800) 541-4871	Windows (floppy disk)	Designed for home and office interior layout; capability to transfer materials list to Design Estimator; includes three-dimensional side views; extensive Symbol libraries.
Autodesk Kitchen and Bath	Autodesk (707) 794-1450	DOS (floppy disk)	Designed for home and office interior layout; extensive CAD capabilities and symbol libraries; includes three-dimensional, elevation, and birdseye views.

Programs You Can Use to Redesign Your Home (Continued)

Program	Manufacturer	Platform	Key Features
3D Virtual Reality Room Planner	COSMI (301) 886-3510	Windows (floppy disk)	Real-time virtual reality walk-through; adjustable ambient light; basic symbols and design elements; east-to-use interface.
3D Home Architect	Broderbund Software, Inc. (800) 521-6263	Windows (CD-ROM)	Multimedia home design software with sections on kitchens and baths; includes three-dimensional layout program with CAD capabilities.
Key Home Designer	Softkey (407) 367-0005	Windows (CD-ROM)	Multimedia home design program with sections on kitchens and baths; includes Key Home Cad, a general-purpose layout program.
Complete House	Deep River Publishing, Inc. (207) 871-1684	Windows (CD-ROM)	Multimedia home design program with sections on kitchens and baths; includes CAD/FP, a general-purpose layout program.

➡ The Case of the Layout Lovebirds

John and Gail had just rented their first apartment and had to decorate it from floor to ceiling. Before making any decorating decisions, they purchased Design Your Own Home Interiors on the recommendation of their computer dealer. They carefully created a layout that matched their apartment, including the placement of doors, windows, appliances, and fixtures. They then experimented with the placement of furniture and the color of walls. Using furniture symbols and side views, they were able to visualize how their apartment would look with different arrangements. They found a layout that was as perfect as their new marriage.

6 Planning *Your* Garden *and* Landscape

Whether

you have a house, condominium, or apartment, your living environment is more than just walls and furniture. Indoor plants and outdoor gardens can enhance your surroundings and improve your quality of life. Decks, patios, and porches can be perfect for entertaining or for quiet moments of contemplation and relaxation.

There are literally thousands of gardening and landscaping resources available to you on your computer. With your computer, you can do all of the following:

- ➡ Get information and how-to help
- ➡ Lay out and design your garden
- ➡ Manage your garden and organize your plants
- ➡ Learn how to plan and design decks and outdoor living areas

Getting How-To Help Online

When you need information on plants or gardens, turn on your computer and access help online.

On America Online, visit the Exchange, where you can share ideas on a variety of topics with other members. In the Exchange window, select the Outdoor Activities button, and then choose Gardening Message Center. From the message center, select a folder that interests you, and then read messages or send your own. You'll find folders on almost every aspect of gardening and landscaping.

On CompuServe you'll find hundreds of messages and files to download in the Garden/Outdoors section of the Dwellings Forum. For more extensive how-to help, check out the Gardening Forum. You'll find over 1,200 files of interest, divided into 21 library areas. For example, search library 2 for articles from *National Gardening* magazine, or browse through section 9 for information on landscape and shrubs. As with all CompuServe forums, you'll find text files, programs, graphics files, and Windows help files.

You can also find garden information and how-to help on the Internet. To get answers to your gardening questions, e-mail your questions to the Garden Hotline

→ Online resources for gardeners

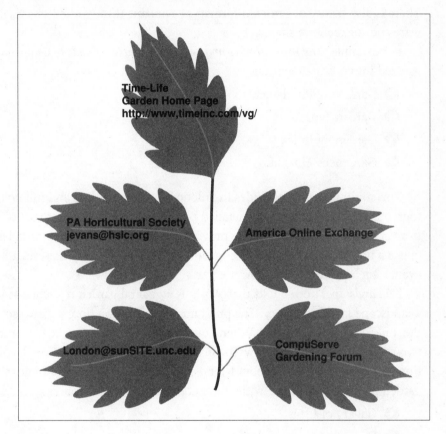

Time-Life
Garden Home Page
http://www.timeinc.com/vg/

PA Horticultural Society
jevans@hslc.org

America Online Exchange

London@sunSITE.unc.edu

CompuServe
Gardening Forum

of the Pennsylvania Horticultural Society at jevans@hslc.org. The society, which sponsors the annual Philadelphia Flower Show, is one of the oldest and most respected horticultural organizations in the country.

If you have a Web browser, try the Time-Life garden home page at http://www.timeinc.com/vg/. From there, you can visit Time-Life's virtual garden database at http://www.timeinc.com/vg/TimeLife/CG/vg-search.html.

For a list of garden-related news groups and FAQs (frequently asked questions), send a message to London@sunSITE.unc.edu. The address reaches the University of North Carolina.

Multimedia Garden Resources

There is also plenty of garden information available through multimedia software and inexpensive shareware.

For example, *The Better Homes and Gardens Complete Guide to Gardening* is organized into four main areas:

- ➜ Gardening Fundamentals
- ➜ Garden Types
- ➜ Gardening Index
- ➜ Gardener's Almanac

This multimedia CD includes instructional how-to videos and full-color photographs. Search the index for detailed plant information on hundreds of plants, from annuals to wildflowers. The program's Gardener's Almanac option lets you create a notebook of your gardening, and it presents monthly tips and a list of events, such as garden and flower shows.

3D Landscape, from Books that Work, is a general garden reference as well as a landscape layout program. The program is supplied on floppy disks, so you don't need a CD-ROM drive. When you start the program, you're presented with two options—Design and How-To Guide. Selecting Design starts the layout function, which you will learn about later. Select How-To-Guide for a multimedia garden reference, complete with animations, in the following areas:

- ➜ Gallery of Ideas
- ➜ Designing Your Landscape
- ➜ Preparing the Site
- ➜ Building Projects
- ➜ Selecting Plants
- ➜ Planting Techniques
- ➜ Rental Tools
- ➜ How To Buy Materials

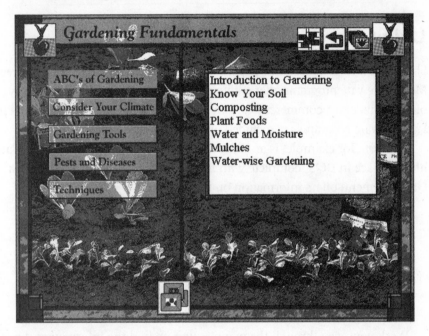

> **Use The Better Homes and Gardens Complete Guide to Gardening to learn about plants and gardening.**

3D Landscape also includes interactive estimators to design your garden for privacy, plan the rough grading, select lawn grass, improve the soil, and estimate concrete to complete a patio or other project.

For additional information, 3D Landscape includes a list of toll-free phone numbers. In addition, each chapter provides access to a manufacturer advertisement. Many of the advertisements are interactive and useful even if you do not buy the product. The advertisement from Rain Bird, for example, helps you create specifications for a sprinkler system. The advertisement from Allan Block estimates the materials you'll need to complete a block retaining or decorative wall.

For a more pictorial garden view, try the *Exotic Garden*. This CD contains 500 color photographs and a time-lapse film named Why Plants Flower. Each photograph includes the flower's botanical name, and information on its planting, growth, and care.

Using Gardening Shareware

Shareware is an excellent way to learn about gardening with a minimal investment. Most shareware programs offer additional features when you register, and you can often upgrade to a commercial version with even more capabilities. Several popular shareware programs are included on the CD accompanying this book.

GrowEm, for example, is an illustrated garden reference that uses a Windows-like interface in DOS, complete with high-quality photographs. The main GrowEm menu offers information on these areas:

- ➡ Propagation Techniques
- ➡ Growth Media and Soil Additives
- ➡ Growth Environment
- ➡ Species Listing by Name
- ➡ Organic Pest Control

Work your way through the menu system to find the information that you need. Selecting Propagation Techniques, for example, will lead to information on starting plants from seeds and cuttings, layering, and grafting.

For each species in its database, the program explains how and when to plant; the best lighting, soil, and temperature conditions; and the recommended planting zone. Illustrations are used to explain topics such as air layering and cutting. If you do not have a CD-ROM drive, download the program from CompuServe's Gardening Forum. Look for the file GROW3V.EXE (874,112 bytes).

Another shareware program on the CD is *The Garden Companion*. While only the first of three menus is available in the shareware program, you still have access to information on 54 annuals and biennials, 108 perennials, 12 border plants, and 106 shrubs, as well as information on lawn care, trees, and other landscape subjects.

For each plant, the program shows the name, genus, height, spread, bloom period, and color. It also recommends climate, light requirements, and soil conditions for each plant. If you do not have a CD-ROM drive, you can download the program from America Online and from the Gardening Forum on Compu-Serve. The file name will depend on the shareware version available at the time. The registered version also contains information on cacti and indoor plants, ground cover, plant propagation, and a wider variety of plants and shrubs.

> *Shareware is an excellent way to learn about gardening with a minimal investment*

Your Database of Plants

If you have a large or varied garden, it may be difficult to remember over the years what you've planted. A good gardener will maintain a record of plants and keep a log of gardening activities, successes, and failures. As with everyone else, a gardener should learn from mistakes.

You can keep the records yourself using a word processing or spreadsheet program. However, a database program is best suited for the task. Using a database program, you can quickly search for specific information and print out informative reports. When you use a program such as Microsoft Access, you can change or add fields to suit your own tastes and needs.

The database form shown here was created with Microsoft Access. This database is included on the CD accompanying this book, in dBase, Excel, and Lotus 1-2-3 formats. The database also includes the Names table, which contains the common and botanical names of 50 plants and tables to record your sources and maintain a log of your activities.

The Microsoft Access database is named PLANTS.MDB. The dBASE, Excel, and Lotus 1-2-3 files have the following names with the appropriate DBF, XLS, and WKS extensions:

- ➡ PLANTS, for recording the plants in your garden
- ➡ VENDORS, for tracking your supplies
- ➡ LOG, for maintaining a record of your activities
- ➡ NAMES, for displaying common and botanical plant names

Gardening database for the green thumb

Use a database to record your garden information and to maintain a log of your activities.

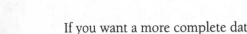
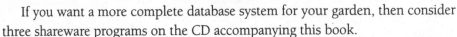

If you want a more complete database system for your garden, then consider three shareware programs on the CD accompanying this book.

Horticultural Manager is a DOS program that lets you maintain a database of the plants in your garden and create a list of tasks for each month of the year. If you do not have a CD-ROM drive, download the file HTMAN_12.ZIP (281265 bytes) from America Online or the file HRTMAN.ZIP from the Garden/Outdoors area of the Dwellings Forum on CompuServe.

Because the program can handle up to 50 separate databases, you can divide your garden into sections or record data for multiple locations. It also includes tables showing the distance to leave between plants and the desired content of nitrogen, phosphorus, and potassium in the soil.

Organize Your Plants and Garden is another DOS database program included on the CD. Use the program to catalog your plants and to keep track of their location in your garden. You can save your database in dBase format, and you can import dBase-formatted files that you have already created. The database form includes 20 fields to record common and botanical names, size, light, growth record, and the supplier from which you purchased the plant.

If you do not have a CD-ROM drive, download the program PLANT558.ZIP (305,135 bytes) from America Online, or the file ORGPLT.ZIP from the Dwellings Forum on CompuServe.

If you prefer Windows, download from the CD the *Multimedia Home Database*, another program from PSG-HomeCraft. This program is actually a complete system that lets you create your own databases. It also includes 11 sample databases that are already designed.

To load the plants database, pull down the File menu and select Catalog Maintenance. A list of the sample databases will appear. Double-click on Plants and then click on OK.

Enter information about a plant into the database, and then click on Save to display a blank database record. Buttons at the top of the screen let you navigate through the database, sort, and search through records. To add a new record, save the one displayed. If a blank record does not appear, click on the Clear button.

For more information on using the program, double-click on the MHD Manual icon in the group. For specific information on the plant database, double-click on the icon labeled Plants.

Recording Your Garden Layout

Even with a database, a graphic layout of your garden is still a necessity. For example, how can you remember the location of each bulb, plant, and flower? You could take the time to place a tag on each plant, but tags can blow away or be damaged by animals. To play it safe, you should have a record of where each plant is located in your garden. Not only will the record help you identify your plants, but it can also help you avoid errors, such as digging up flower bulbs that you really want to leave in place for the next blooming season.

The easiest way to keep track of plant location is to draw a sketch of your layout. You can draw it on paper, but the drawing becomes cluttered as you add, remove, and replant objects in your garden.

An easier way is to use Windows Paintbrush to create a sketch of your garden. Use the drawing tools to sketch the overall plot area. Use the line or rectangle tools if the lot borders are straight, or use the freehand, arch, or ellipse tools if the border is irregular.

Next, draw any structures in the garden that will not move, such as fences, pools, benches, and arbors.

➡ Use Paintbrush to record your garden's layout.

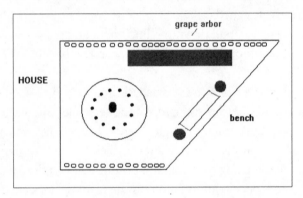

If you cannot remember the placement of plants, save the drawing, print out a copy, and take it out to the garden. Draw in the plant layout by hand and then go back to your computer. Now draw the individual plants, using the ellipse tool to quickly indicate trees, bushes, and shrubs. You can use the freehand tool or the spray tool to draw in ground cover and sections of small plants and flowers. With the text tool, enter the name of each plant in the garden. Save and print the drawing again. As you change your garden, indicate the changes by hand on the copy and later change the electronic copy when you have time. Use the Save As command to save each version of the sketch. This will leave the previous sketch unchanged. By retaining previous sketches, you can print out copies of each variation to visualize the way your garden has grown and changed over a period of time.

Planning Your Landscape Design

Paintbrush is just one tool that you can use to maintain a layout of your garden. You can also use some of the layout programs discussed in previous chapters. *Planix Home*, for example, includes hundreds of symbols for outdoor layout, including recreation objects such as pools and barbeques, sprinklers, and 42 symbols for trees and plants.

However, your computer can be used for much more than merely recording a layout of your current garden. By using specialized layout programs, you can plan and design every aspect of your garden and landscape. Landscape design programs include many of the CAD features found in more general-purpose layout programs. They also include symbols for trees, shrubs, and plants, as well as outdoor furniture, driveways, and other exterior features.

Many landscape programs go far beyond these basics with features like these:

- ➔ A database that helps you select the proper plants for your geographic area
- ➔ A growth feature to illustrate how your garden will appear in the future
- ➔ A shading function to show how your house and garden cast shadows
- ➔ Slope and elevation functions for matching the slope of your property

You can evaluate landscape design programs much as you do general-purpose layout programs. Some landscape programs are more CAD-oriented, with details and options for very precise placement of objects. Others are more intuitive, with color and three-dimensional views to encourage creativity.

The Landscape Designer section of 3D Landscape, for example, provides both top and three-dimensional views as well as a slope editor. This Windows program has a very easy interface. All of its symbols, for example, are easily accessed through a virtual spiral-bound book on the screen. You select the tab of the book to display a page of related symbols, and then click on the symbol for the object you want to insert.

Select all symbols from a virtual spiral-bound book. The symbols are categorized into lot, house, trees, shrubs, plants, projects, structures, utilities, and other.

To start working on your layout, select the property line symbol from the lot tab and then drag the mouse to create a rectangle the size of your lot. As you

⊙ Design a professional-looking garden.

Use a landscape design program such as LandDesigner to lay out a professional-looking garden.

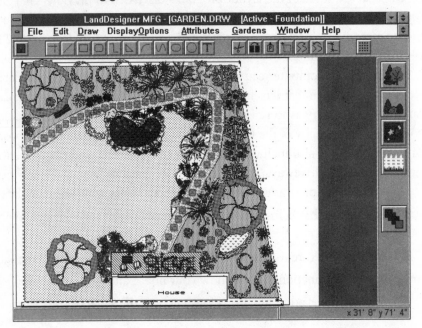

drag, the dimensions of the lot appear in the status bar. You can drag individual points around most symbols to modify their shape. So if your lot isn't rectangular, just drag the appropriate point along the property line to modify its shape.

You can indicate the location of your house just as easily. Select the house symbol from the house tab, and then drag the mouse to create a rectangular shape. Drag points around the rectangle to create L-shaped, U-shaped, and other house configurations.

Next, add plants to the layout. The plant and tree symbols include a series of generic shapes. You select a shape that matches that of the plant you want to indicate, and then you insert the symbol into the layout. You then assign that instance of the symbol to one of 350 specific plants in the database. The program makes it easy to assign the plant by giving you the option of limiting the search to plants with that shape or that match local condition.

Once you complete your layout, you can generate a list of materials, complete with estimated costs. Each of the built-in plants, and most of the other provided objects, are assigned a cost based on the national average. You can change the cost maintained by the database if your local price differs.

The database for construction objects, such as fences, patios, and walkways, is extensive. When you add a fence, for example, you can designate its type— picket, board, wood rail, or chain link. The program then reports all of the materials you'll need for the project, including details such as number, size, and type of nails.

The program also provides a Growth Over Time feature. You indicate a year in the future, and the program adjusts the sizes of plants to show their spacing at that time. There is also a Shadow Caster option to illustrate how shadows appear during all times of the day.

Books That Work also has two other programs for the gardener:

- ➡ *Garden Plant Selector* lets you see descriptions and planting information on over 400 plants.

- ➡ *Landscape Backyard Construction* presents how-to instructions and tips from pros on over 30 landscaping projects, such as building retaining walls and fences.

Design Your Own Landscape, from Abracadata, uses the same overall interface as Design Your Own Interior, including plan and three-dimensional side views. It also has an age feature to see how your plants will appear in the future.

The program has an extensive library of hundreds of symbols in 18 categories. In addition to a wide variety of plants and trees, the library includes symbols for designing the exterior view of your house, such as chimneys, doors, and windows. There is even a library of houses, giving you basic house layouts at the click of a mouse. In addition, you can create your own symbols and libraries, and you can edit the database of plant symbols.

As with other Abracadata products, you can export a materials list from Design Your Own Landscape to the Design Estimator for producing cost estimates

Avoid a jungle in your yard.

Landscape programs, such as Design Your Own Landscape, can show how your garden will appear over time.

1 year

3 years

6 years

and budgets. Design Your Own Landscape, however, does not maintain any pricing information.

While Design Your Own Landscape lacks CAD features that may be required for a professional landscaper, it is easy and fun to use and does not require a CD-ROM drive. It is a good choice if you want to do a simple layout of both your house and garden.

Land Designer, a CD from Green Thumb software, includes many CAD-like functions, such as snap-to grid drawing and layers. It includes symbols for trees, shrubs, plants, and ground cover, as well as objects such as pools, fences, walkways, and so forth. Its plant database includes extensive, detailed information, and you can edit and add your own information as well.

As with 3D Landscape, you add a plant using a generic symbol, and then associate it with a specific item from the database. Some database items are already associated with prices that appear when you generate a materials list and order form. You can display a form for each plant listing its type, spacing, depth, and price. You can also display a full-color photograph of each plant and hear its correct pronunciation.

The program's layer feature lets you control what elements appear on the screen and on the materials list. There are 12 predefined layers. For example, you can use the spring, summer, fall, and winter layers to visualize your garden in the various seasons. Land Designer, with its CAD features for landscape design, is more suitable for the serious gardener and professional landscaper.

You'll find a comprehensive demonstration and tutorial about LandDesigner on the CD accompanying this book. You can get a quick screen tour of the program, learn how to start your garden plan, and learn how to add garden elements to the plan. You'll also learn how to select plants and other materials, as well as how to use the program's multimedia features.

Finally, *AutoDesk Landscape* is a DOS-based layout program supplied on floppy disk. It has the same interface as AutoDesk Home and AutoDesk Kitchen and Bath, with plan, birdseye, and three-dimensional views. Its roots are definitely in CAD—its extensive layout capabilities and features make it suitable for the professional landscaper or sprinkler contractor. There are symbols for objects to complete the outdoor environment—doors, windows, outdoor games, fences, and furniture. Plant symbols, however, are generic. There is no database of planting information, photographs, or other elements for the home gardener. When you add a shopping list to the drawing, plants are listed by their overall type—such as deciduous shrub or evergreen tree—although you can edit the text to insert specific plants.

Planning Your Vegetable Garden

Vegetable gardens have their own set of requirements, so it is not surprising that there are special layout programs devoted entirely to them.

Sprout is Abracadata's layout program for vegetable gardens. It offers the same layout capabilities as Design Your Own Landscape, but without the three-dimensional side views. When you select a plant and add it to the layout, the program will automatically insert the symbols into rows at the proper spacing. It has an extensive database on vegetables, including information such as:

- Planting time
- Germination days
- Harvest time
- Soil pH
- Plants needed to produce food for one person
- Spacing of seeds, plants, and rows
- Planting depth

You can add your own symbols and planting data, and you can edit the database if needed. The printed manual includes a section of growing tips for 80 vegetables.

Garden Assistant is a shareware program under DOS that lets you create a plot diagram of your vegetable garden. You can download the program as GAR-DASST.ZIP (173,309 bytes) from America Online or from CompuServe as file GASSIS.ARC in the Gardening Forum. You can also order the registered version directly from Shannon Software and Zephyr Services.

If you enter the number of people you want to feed with your produce, the program will calculate the number of row feet and the number of plants, and it will lay out your garden for you.

The program includes two useful tables. One table lists the plant and harvest dates for each vegetable. The Vegetable Parameters Table lists these details:

- Name
- Row feet per person to feed
- Quantity for each 100 feet
- Plant depth
- Distance between each row
- Vegetable group
- Minimum number of rows to be planted
- Maximum row length

Entertaining Outdoors with Decks

Your landscape design might also call for a deck. Rather than use a general purpose layout program, consider one of these programs.

Deck: The Home Series from AutoDesk uses the same interface as other AutoDesk layout programs. It lets you create your deck in two-dimensional plan view and then display it in birdseye or eye-level three-dimensional view.

Design and Build Your Deck, from Books That Work is a multimedia guide to deck building with top, three-dimensional and side views. It includes over 40 full-color animations with sound.

Safety, Security, and the Automated Home

No matter where you live, the world can be a cruel place. Through theft, fire, flood, or some other disaster, you could lose valuable possessions and sentimental personal items. One way to deal with property loss is to know exactly what you have by taking a personal property inventory. The inventory will be invaluable when you're making insurance claims since you'll be able to determine exactly what has been stolen, lost, or destroyed. But why wait for disaster to strike? You can help to prevent property loss and damage by automating your home. And of course, your computer can do it all!

Your Personal Inventory

Taking an inventory of your possessions is really easy. You'll need to go through each room of your house, recording information about your possessions. You can use the database on the CD accompanying this book for your home inventory. You'll find it in Access and dBASE format, as well as in Excel and Lotus 1-2-3. Or you can create your own database. Create a database with each item of information as a separate field, as shown here. (Using a spreadsheet program, each item would be a column heading.)

Gather together any receipts or insurance appraisals that you have. Go through each room of your house carefully, cataloging each item that has any value to you. (Don't forget sentimental items that have no intrinsic worth—you can use these when writing bequeathals in your will.)

If you have a laptop or notebook computer, take it with you as you go room by room cataloging your possessions. Otherwise, print out copies of your worksheet or database form to record the information and later transcribe the data into your computer program.

You can use the database on the CD accompanying this book for your home inventory

You can later sort the records by location, type, or any other item. Recording the type of item is very useful. Most insurance policies have limits of coverage on items such as computers, cameras, and jewelry. If you sort by type and add subtotals of their values, you can make sure you have enough extra coverage for your valuables.

Use a database to record your home inventory information.

This home inventory database, included on the CD, was created with the Microsoft Access Table Wizard.

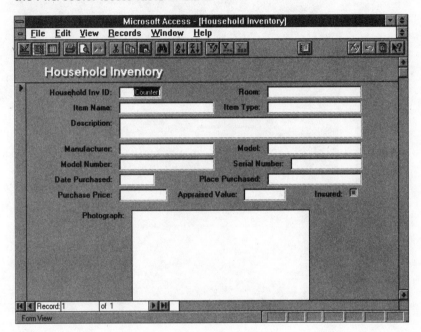

Home Inventory Software

Rather than create a worksheet or database yourself, try out four shareware programs that are included on the CD accompanying this book. You'll find two programs for DOS and two for Windows, so you can take your pick.

SmartTracker is a Windows program that lets you display inventory information in columns, much like a worksheet, or in individual forms. As with a worksheet, you can adjust the width and order of columns, and you can select which columns to display on screen.

By default, not all of the available fields will be shown in columns on screen. To select which fields to display and to adjust their order and width, click on the Viewer button in the program's main window. From the Viewer window, shown here, you make your adjustments to select and order the fields.

Take your home inventory with SmartTracker.

SmartTracker lets you select which fields appear in the inventory and change their order.

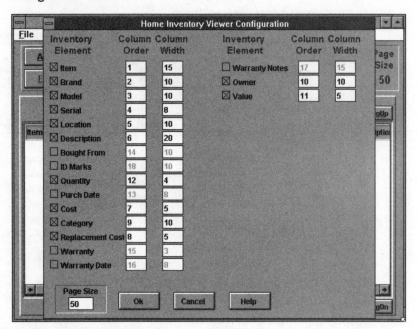

You can add and edit information on a convenient Inventory Item Input form. The form displays text boxes for all of the database fields, and it includes list boxes that allow you to select from 27 home locations and 14 item categories. You can even add your own locations and categories to the lists.

The program allows a wide range of report forms. You can sort reports by item, location, category, or owner. You can also select from five form options:

➤ A *single line form* includes each item name, location, owner, cost and replacement cost.

➤ A *two line form* also includes the brand name, model, serial number, and warranty data.

➤ The *full description* contains all of the fields in seven lines of data for each item.

➡ A *value summary* report shows only the cost, value, and replacement cost, with group totals and grand totals.

➡ A *user defined* report lets you to create your own format.

For insurance purposes you can also add to each report the name of the insurance company and policy number, as well as an inventory statement. In the statement, you attest that the inventory list is correct as of the date printed. There is also an option to export the report to a data file and to import a text file into the database.

In Chapter 6 you learned how to use Multimedia Home Database to record information about your garden. The program also includes databases for tracking these items:

➡ Artwork

➡ Fabric

➡ Guns

➡ Personal possessions

➡ Mail

➡ Memorabilia

➡ Model railroad inventory

➡ Photographs

➡ Recipes

➡ Wine

Once you run Multimedia Home Database, pull down the File menu and select Catalog Maintenance. Double-click on the database you want to use and then click on OK.

You can customize any of the databases or create your own from the Catalog Maintenance dialog box. To customize a database, select it and then click on the Change Format button. To create your own database, click on the New button. You can name up to 21 fields as well as multiple keys. You can also have the program automatically maintain running totals of numeric fields.

You can also insert sound and bitmap files into fields. The program will even display a thumbnail sketch of the bitmap on the screen. The only limitation is that the bitmap and sound files must be on the same directory as the program itself.

Reports are easy to set up, with plenty of options. You can design and save multiple reports for each database. A graphics editor lets you insert and position the fields so you can design columnar reports, mailing labels, or forms.

If you prefer a DOS interface, consider either Around the House or Organize! Your Home, both of which are on the CD.

Around the House is a general-purpose program designed to manage your home records. It organizes databases into two major categories according to your lifestyle rather than by possessions—All My Files and Where My Money Goes. Under All My Files, you can select these formats:

- Who I know
- What I have
- My appointments
- All my notes
- Letters and stuff
- Grocery list
- To Do List

The Where My Money Goes category includes these items:

- What I make
- Money going out
- What's left
- My vehicles
- My house
- Cost of groceries
- Contributions and donations

There are five built-in report formats; you can also create your own custom report.

For your home inventory, select the What I Have option. The database form lets you enter the details of each item, as well as select from a list of categories and locations.

Organize! Your Home is the DOS equivalent of the home inventory database of Multimedia Home Database, but without the sound and graphics files. It uses the same general interface as Organize Your Plants and Garden (described in Chapter 6).

The program is unique in this class because it provides three levels of security:

➔ Level 1 allows access only to users who know the security code that you specify.

➔ Level 2 allows full access to anyone who knows the security code and read-only access to everyone else.

➔ Level 3 provides complete access to anyone.

With Organize! Your Home you create any number of databases to store categories of information. Each database, called a catalog, can have a different format. When you define a catalog, you name and index fields, and you can also select fields to be totaled. User-defined calculated fields can contain a formula using other fields as values.

Safety and Automation

Having a complete record of your home's contents can help you deal with property loss but it cannot prevent it. But don't despair—you can also use your computer to control and monitor your home's lights, appliances, and alarm system to help prevent property loss in the first place.

The most popular automation systems use the X10 family of products. The X10 system was invented by a company named X10 Powerhouse, but compatible products are sold by many companies, including Radio Shack.

The X10 system consists of modules that control individual lights, switches, appliances, and other electronic equipment. For example, to control a light in your living room, you plug an X10 lamp module into a wall outlet, and then plug the lamp into the module. To control your coffeepot in the kitchen, plug an appliance module into the outlet and then plug the coffee pot into the module.

Setting up an X10 system

Connecting an X10 control system is as easy as plugging in an appliance.

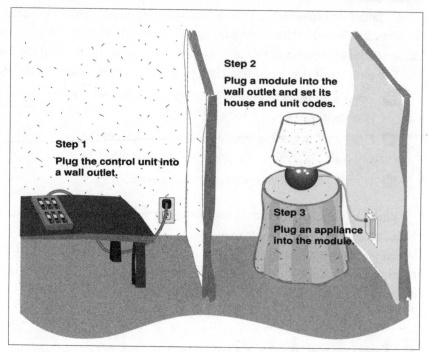

Step 2

Plug a module into the wall outlet and set its house and unit codes.

Step 1

Plug the control unit into a wall outlet.

Step 3

Plug an appliance into the module.

Every module includes two switches. You use the switches to identify the module by house code (from A to P) and unit code (1 to 16). For example, the living room light might be module A1, the coffeepot module M16. In addition to lamp and appliance modules that plug into outlets, there are modules for wall switches and dimmers, wall outlets, heavy duty air conditioners, and low voltage circuits. There are even wireless wall switches that you use to control a circuit using a switch without installing new wiring.

You use a variety of control devices to remotely turn on or off each unit or to dim lights. Just plug the control unit into any wall outlet and it is ready. The control unit lets you select the house and unit code for the module you want to control. For example, if you have the control box near your bed, you can turn on the coffeepot when you wake up in the morning by indicating *module M16* and then pressing a switch.

You do not need to connect the controller to the units. Every component must be plugged into a regular wall outlet, and the signals to control units pass through your home's electrical wiring.

Rather than manually controlling units using switches, you can use your computer to automate the task. A device called the CP-290 Powerhouse Interface connects to your computer's serial port. You then use one of a variety of computer programs to create a series of events, such as:

- Turn on the porch light at sundown
- Turn off the porch light at 3 a.m.
- Turn on the coffee pot at 8 a.m.

When you install the software on your system, you indicate the longitude and latitude of your location. The program then calculates sundown and sunset times for you.

The software downloads the events into the CP-290's internal memory. You can then turn off your computer. The CP-290 transmits the commands to the modules at the appropriate times. Each CP-290 can control up to 256 modules.

You can purchase the CP-290 by itself or with software from a variety of vendors. The features of the software vary. Deskmate software from Radio Shack, for example, lets you draw a layout of your home and indicate the position and codes of modules while many other programs do not.

Plato for Windows software, available from most X10 vendors, goes even further. Plato lets you add floor plans, photographs, and three-dimensional drawings for virtual reality graphics. There is even a version of Plato that monitors the state of X10 modules—reporting which lights are on and which are off, for example.

You can download from America Online a shareware version of Plato as the file X10MSW30.EXE. If you do not have the CP-290 connected to your computer, the program runs in demonstration mode to illustrate its features. The shareware version lets you program on and off times for each module. You can define events using days of the week, months, and even seasons.

Use your computer to automate your X10 system.

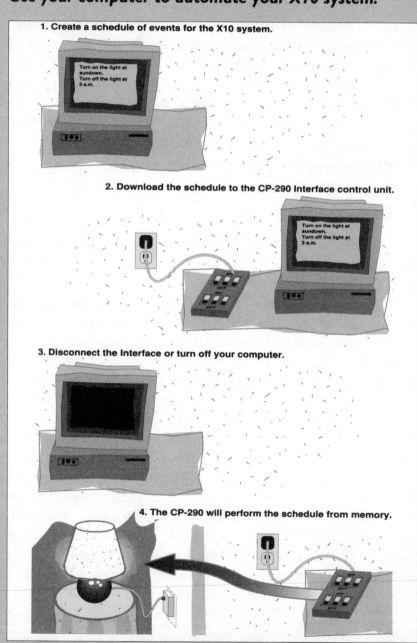

1. Create a schedule of events for the X10 system.

Turn on the light at sundown.
Turn off the light at 3 a.m.

2. Download the schedule to the CP-290 Interface control unit.

Turn on the light at sundown.
Turn off the light at 3 a.m.

3. Disconnect the Interface or turn off your computer.

4. The CP-290 will perform the schedule from memory.

Plato for Windows: A full-featured home automation program

Plato, and its shareware version X10MSW, let you program X10 events using days, months, and seasons.

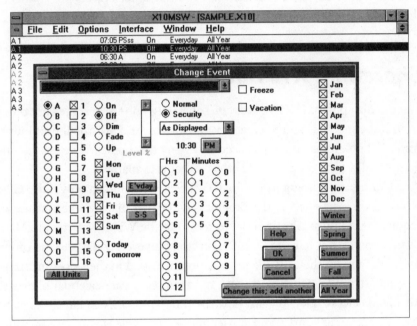

If you don't want to assemble an automation system yourself, you can purchase modules, the CP-290 interface, and software as a set. Starter sets are usually available for under $130. For a complete catalog of X10 products, contact Home Automation Systems at 1-800-762-7846.

While the CP-290 is the most popular controller for X10 systems, it is not the only one available. The ES-1400e from Enerlogic Systems, for example, includes a more advanced PC interface and controller. The system uses a special module that decodes and transmits X10 commands through the power line. In addition to sending commands to X10 modules, the system monitors their status. If you have door or window security sensors, for example, the controller can detect if a door or window is open and take the appropriate action. The controller also senses when you use a remote module to turn an X10 device on or off. The ES-1400e comes with comprehensive software, including a viewer program that displays the status of all X10 objects in your system. You can even expand the system with a telephone interface to allow remote command of the controller through a modem, and to use infrared controllers for objects not connected to the power line.

Shareware X10 Automation Programs

You can also purchase X10 hardware separately, and use a shareware program to control the modules and to create events for the CP-290. You'll find four shareware X10 programs on the CD accompanying this book. We've selected the programs to illustrate the range of software that is available.

All of the X10 programs on the CD except one will run only if the CP-290 interface is on your system. The programs will either display an error message or require you to press Alt+Ctrl+Del to return to the Windows Program Manager. Even if you do not have a CP-290 interface, however, you'll find the programs useful because of the valuable information provided in their documentation.

Smart10 is a DOS program that can maintain a year's calendar of events. Read the file SMART10.TXT to learn how the program works. Smart10 can schedule events to occur at sunrise and sunset and between dates you have specified. You enter latitude, longitude, and time zone information to set sunrise and sunset parameters. The program includes a text file—Location.TXT—that contains the longitude and latitude for over 1,000 cities worldwide. A Smart10 schedule might look like this:

```
Sue's Work Room: Light Switch #C1
  on ~10:00 pm everyday
  off ~11:30 pm if not someone visiting
weekdays
  off ~12:00 am if not someone visiting
weekends

Family Room: Track Lights #B1
  off @ sunrise everyday
```

```
off ~11:00 pm everyday

Living Room: Light Switch #B8
  off @ sunrise everyday
  dim 80% ~ sunset-15 everyday
  off ~11:30 pm if not someone out every
day

Study: LaserJet #A3
  off @ 2:00 am every day
```

X10CTL is a Windows CP-290 control program. Timed events in a schedule can use references such as Today, Tomorrow, Everyday, Weekdays, or Weekends, and events can be based on sunrise or sunset times. There is a 16-position dimmer function for lamp units or light switches. You'll find information on how to use this program in the file X10CTL26.WRI. Open the file in Windows Write, Word for Windows, or another program that reads Write-formatted files.

X10DC Direct Control is also a DOS program. Rather than downloading a schedule, it allows commands to be executed immediately by the CP290. A Command History list box stores up to 1,000 commands. Documentation on the program is in the file X10DC.DOC. This is one program that you can start even if you do not have the controller. When you run it, a box appears warning that the controller cannot be located. Select Cancel to see the main screen.

Finally, *XA* is a command-line interpreter that works from the DOS prompt. You define each of your units in a file called XA.INI, such as

```
define Deck_Lights     a1
define Bedroom_Light   a2
```

You can then enter commands from the DOS prompt, such as XA Deck_Lights OFF and Bedroom_Light ON.

You can execute multiple commands in batch files or text files. The file US_LATIT.TXT contains longitudes and latitudes of cities in all 50 U.S. states.

X10DC Direct Control

The X10DC program lets you define each X10 unit by its location.

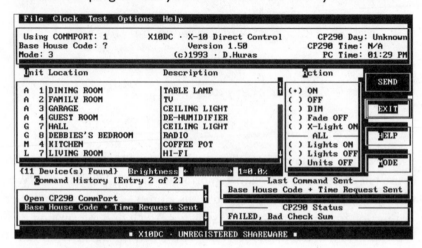

The CEBus Interface

In addition to the X10 protocol, you can also create an automated system using a newer standard, *CEBus*. This standard was developed under the sponsorship of the Electronics Industries Association to allow creation of a system that would integrate all of your home appliances. Connections can be made through the power line, as with X10, as well as through telephone and video wiring and by wireless transmission.

Using CEBus, for example, you can connect your television to your home security system. In fact, you can create a network connecting all of your home electronic products, including X10 devices.

The CEBus features a two-way communication path. Not only can it send commands to modules, but it can receive input from sensors as well. The system is based on an interface card that fits inside your computer, or within a separate universal controller. Messages from sensors throughout your house tell the system how to react.

A CEBus system from Unity System, for example, can control alarm systems, appliances, and communications equipment as well as dampers and valves to control the flow of water and air in heating and cooling equipment. Sensors feed back to your computer information on your home's environment, such as temperature, humidity, smoke, heat, and alarm input.

The X10 system relies on your computer's serial port for one-way communications. The CEBus system uses its own interface for both input and output. The *AUTOMATE* shareware program on the CD accompanying this book describes a unique system of control through the computer's game card or parallel port. The shareware version is a reference and demonstration of the system.

The registered version gives you detailed how-to information for designing your own system, and tells you where to purchase the necessary hardware. It also includes a collection of handy programs to use once your system is developed.

The AUTOMATE system allows your computer to monitor your environment, sending signals to X10 and other devices as appropriate. Aspects monitored include

- Light
- Humidity
- Temperature
- Wind speed
- Wind direction
- Moisture
- Vibration
- Pressure
- Heat
- Motion
- Levels (such as of tubs or tanks)
- Weight
- Time

For more information about home automation, look through the Home Automation section of CompuServe's Family Handyman Forum, or the Lighting\Automation section of the Dwellings Forum.

Faux Control

Home security and automation systems will obviously cost you some money. For a taste of home security on a budget, download the program *HOFF* from either America Online or CompuServe. On America Online, download the file HOFF120A.ZIP (81,779 bytes) from the software libraries. From CompuServe, download HOFF.ZIP from the Safety/Security section of the Dwellings Forum.

HOFF contains the ALARM program, which keeps people away from your computer and the area around it. When you run ALARM, you are asked to position your mouse in an unstable position—where it would move if someone knocked into your table or opened a drawer. Your screen changes to a fictitious display of financial information. If someone presses a key, moves the mouse, or even shakes the table enough to move the mouse, a siren sounds and an alert message flashes across the screen. Just look for red faces if you use ALARM on your office computer.

➲ The Case of Lucky Lou

Louellen and Don completely automated their home using a CEBus system. The expense seemed frivolous to their friends and family and was a constant source of good-natured teasing—that is, until one day in January when Louellen and Don were on a ski vacation. Don had programmed their system to place a series of phone calls if the controller detected any problem. Louellen's mother received a call in which a recorded voice reported that water had been detected in her daughter's home. She called the plumber, who quickly found and repaired a burst water pipe. If the automated system had not detected the leak, Louellen and Don would have returned to a very messy and expensive problem.

Appendix A: How to Use the CD-ROM

The CD-ROM accompanying this book can make improving your home with your computer even easier! Included are many of the shareware programs discussed throughout the book, as well as all of the worksheets and databases illustrated in the text, your online connection to CompuServe via WinCIM, information about other Ziff-Davis books, and more. Here's what you need to use the CD:

- IBM-Compatible PC
- 386DX-33 (486DX-33 or faster recommended)
- 4MB RAM (minimum)
- 4MB available on your hard drive
- Super VGA adapter (supporting 640-by-480 resolution and 256) colors highly recommended
- Microsoft mouse or 100-percent compatible
- Microsoft Windows 3.1 or higher
- Single-speed CD-ROM drive (double-speed recommended)

Installing the CD

To install the Home Improvement icon on your desktop in the Ziff-Davis Press program group, go to File Manager and select Run from the File menu. Click on the Browse button to display a dialog box, pull down the Drives list, and then select the drive representing your CD-ROM. Double-click on INSTALL.EXE in the File Name list. (Don't forget to read the README file that appears in the program group.)

To run the CD directly without installing it on your desktop, follow the same instructions but double-click on RUN_ME.EXE in the File Name list.

Accessing the Files on the CD

When you start the CD, you will see eight options listed on the screen:

- Planning Improvements
- Designing and Building Your Home
- How-To Help
- Garden and Landcape
- Safety, Security, and the Automated Home
- Financial Improvement
- Online Service
- More from Ziff-Davis Press

To use the demos, shareware, and worksheets on the CD, you must first download them to your computer. To do this:

1. Click on one of the categories on the main screen.

2. Double-click on the name of the program or worksheet that you want to download, or highlight the name and click on the Install icon. You'll see a dialog box showing the default download directory. (A few programs install or run directly from the CD when you double-click on their names.)

3. Click on OK to accept the directory shown—make a note of it so you can access the file later. By default the directory will be created within the ZDHOME directory. (If you do not want to use the default directory, enter your own before clicking on OK.)

4. Exit the CD and return to Program Manager.

5. Select Run from the File menu and click on Browse.

6. Double-click on the directory where you downloaded the program, and then double-click on the name that appears in the File Name list.

This will create a series of files in that directory, or in another directory that will be shown on the screen. In most cases you can now run the program using the File, Run command, or by returning to the DOS prompt and running the program from there. In other cases you must install or set up the program before you can run it. Look for a program called INSTALL.EXE or SETUP.EXE in the directory and double-click on it to prepare the program for your use.

Here's the shareware that you'll find on the CD:

Planning Improvements

Mini FEET INCH Dimensional Calculator lets you compute square feet and other calculations by entering measurements in feet, inches, and fractions. Running SETUP.EXE will create a group named Mini FEET in your Windows desktop. Open the group and double-click on the icon labeled *Mini Ft.In.* (Copyright Claw Software)

Handyman Conversions calculates the amount of materials needed to complete typical home improvement projects. Once the program is installed, run HANDYMAN.EXE. (Copyright 1992—Dennis E. Auston)

Home Loan Diary lets you maintain records of payments for home improvement loans and mortgages. After installing the program, start it by running LOAN.EXE. (Copyright 1992–1995 by Philip P. Kapusta)

Remodel Estimator prepares estimates for home improvement projects. Run REMODEL.EXE to create your estimate. (Remodel Estimator © CPR International, 1995)

Designing and Building Your Home

FloorPlan 3D Plus is a working demonstration of this popular layout and design program. To install the demonstration version, you'll need Windows 3.1 or higher, at least 2MB of hard disk space, and 4MB of memory. When you double-click on the demo to unload it, a dialog box will appear informing you that it is temporarily leaving the program to install FloorPlan 3D Plus. Click on OK. This will cause the program to install and a program group to appear on your desktop. To run the program, open the group and double-click on the FloorPlan 3D Plus icon.

Home Inspector for DOS teaches you how to inspect prospective homes and home improvement projects, such as additions. To start the program, go to its directory and run INSPECT.EXE. (Copyright © 1995 North Shore Home Inspections)

Home Inspector for Windows is a demonstration of the commercial version of the program for Windows. After installing the program, execute INSDEMO.EXE. (Copyright © 1995 North Shore Home Inspections)

HomePlan for DOS is a layout and design shareware program. Once the files have been set up on your disk, run HOMEPLN.EXE to use the program. (Copyright 1994 by Chuck Herndon)

Design-A-Room for Windows is a layout and design shareware program. Run SETUP.EXE to install the program and to create a Program Manager group called Design-A-Room. Open the group and double-click on the icon that appears. (Copyright 1994 Robert Scott Mace and Robert A. Mace)

What Should You Expect from Your Architect and **Finding the Architect of Your Dreams** are text files that will help you plan new home construction and major improvements. Install the files from the CD and then open them into any word processing program. Files provided by Martin Butcher CompuServe 100100,1703), an architect and urban planner who is currently developing an online design service.

How-To Help

Your Electrical Reference Source gives you detailed information on electrical wiring, home repair, and new installations. After you install the program, use the File Run command in Program Manager to run 1SASW.HLP. (Copyright 1994, 1995, Roger C. Altman)

Joy's Hints and Tips is a collection of useful information on a wide variety of household and home improvement topics. Run HINTS.EXE. (Copyright © 1995 by Gayle Hughes and available from Joys Software)

LandDesigner from GreenThumb Software is a tutorial on using this landscape design program. To start the tutorial, double-click on its name in the list; then click on OK when the dialog box appears informing you that you are temporarily leaving the program.

GrowEm is an illustrated garden reference with information on propagation techniques, growth media, soil additives, the growing environment, details on plants, and organic pest control. Run the program by starting GROW.EXE. (Copyright © 1995, Paul Postumo. All rights reserved.)

Garden Companion contains detailed information on annuals and biennials, perennials, border plants, shrubs, lawn care, trees, and other landscape subjects. Start the program by running GARDEN19.EXE. (Copyright Bill Hammond 1995)

Horticultural Manager lets you maintain a database of the plants in your garden and composes a list of tasks for each month of the year. It also includes tables showing the distance to leave between plants and the desired nutritional soil content of nitrogen, phosphorus, and potassium. To start the program, run HORTMAN.EXE. (Copyright 1994–1995 Sunrise Software)

Organize Your Plants and Gardens for DOS lets you catalog your plants and keep track of their location in your garden. Run the program by clicking on OYC.EXE. (Copyright 1991, 1992, 1993, 1994, 1995 by H.C.P. Services, Inc.)

Multimedia Home Database for Windows is a complete system that lets you create your own databases. It includes eleven sample databases that are already designed. Installing the program will create a Program Manager group named Multimedia Home Database. To run the program, open the group and double-click on the icon with the same name. (Copyright 1991, 1992, 1993, 1994, 1995 by H.C.P. Services, Inc.)

Safety, Security, and the Automated Home

SmartTracker Inventory is a windows program that lets you maintain your household inventory. You can customize the display of information and select from 27 locations and 14 categories. Installing the program with SETUP.EXE will create a Program Manager group called ISS Collection Series. To run the program, open the group and double-click on the icon labeled *SmartTracker Inventory*. (Copyright 1994, 1995 Insight Software Solutions: Author Michael D. Jones)

Around the House is a general-purpose program to manage your home records, organized into two lifestyle categories: All My Files and Where My Money Goes. After you install the program, run ATH.EXE. (Around the House © 1991, 1994 by BlueCollar Software; all rights reserved.)

Organize! Your Home lets you maintain an inventory of your possessions and print reports. To use the program, run OYH.EXE. (Copyright 1991, 1992, 1993, 1994, 1995 by H.C.P. Services, Inc.)

X10CTL26 is a Windows CP-290 control program to help you automate your home. Events can be offset from sunrise or sunset, and there is a 16-position dimmer function for lamp units or light switches. After you install the program with X10Setup.EXE, read the file X10CTL26.WRI. (This program is distributed freeware in Microsoft Visual Basic 2.0. Portions © 1992, Microsoft Corporation)

X10DC lets you give immediate commands to be executed by the CP-290. To run the program, double-click on X10DC.EXE. If you do not have the controller attached to your computer, select Cancel from the dialog box that will appear.(Copyright 1993–1995 D. Huras)

X10A3 is a command-line interpreter that works from the DOS prompt to give commands to the CP-290 controller. Run XA.EXE for an on-screen manual. (The XA software package, including its documentation and utilities is Copyright © 1991–1995 by Bruce Christian. All Rights Reserved)

AUTOMATE is a tutorial and demonstration program for using parallel and game ports to monitor your environment, sending signals to X10 and other devices. Run AUTOMATE.EXE to start the demonstration. (AUTOMATE Shareware is part of the Automate Project. It may be freely distributed in its exact full and complete form without restrictions.)

Smart10 is a DOS CP-290 program that can maintain a year's calendar of events. Read the file SMART10.TXT to learn how the program works. The file LOCATION.TXT contains the longitude and latitude for over 1,000 cities. (Copyright © 1991-1994 by Sympathetic Software)

Financial Improvement

The Smart Homeowner will help you choose between buying and renting, determine how much you can afford and how much you can save by making extra payments, and decide on the merits of refinancing. Start HOME.EXE to run the program. (Copyright IEG Consultants, Inc.)

The Mortgage Analyzer displays amortization schedules and loan qualification, and compares refinancing options, buying versus renting, and leasing versus selling. Run MORT.EXE to try out the program. (Copyright 1992, 1994 Insight Software Solutions. Author: Michael D. Jones.)

QualifyR Windows computes monthly principal and interest, downpayment amounts, total purchase cost, total due at closing, loan amount, loan-to-value ratio, and minimum monthly income required. Extracting the program files will create a directory named QUALIFYR. From that directory, run SETUP.EXE to create a Program Manager group named QUALIFYR. Open the group and double-click on the program icon. (Copyright 1994, Jeffrey L. Gates)

Analyze Loan Qualification Worksheet and **AMORT** Excel macro by David Grimmer generate amortization schedules. Start Excel and open the worksheet and macro. (Copyright 1995 Ohio Star Software)

Master Amoritiser creates tables comparing mortgages, charts that compare monthly payment and total amount paid for mortgages of different durations, and amortization schedules. It lets you review the effect of increasing payments and the balance of the loan at the end of any period, and it lets you make minor payment adjustments. Run AMORTC.EXE to calculate loan payments. Run AMORTW.EXE for complete amortization information. (Copyright 1992–1995 by Dan Norman. All rights reserved)

Mortgage Designer graphically illustrates amortization information, supports extra payments, and can perform "what-if" analysis by varying principle, interest, term, or payments, by filling in the missing variable. Installing the program creates a program group called MaeDae Shareware. Open the group and double-click on the icon for Mortgage Design. (Copyright MaeDae Enterprises)

House Mouse calculates mortgage information and displays data on payment, interest, and equity in a graphical format. You can save the data in spreadsheet format. Setting up the program creates a group called MH2. Open the group and double-click on the icon for HM2. (Copyright 1994 by Kestrel Computing Company, Inc.)

Loan Arranger, by Fred Schipp, performs mortgage calculations and stores information on multiple loans. It can also determine the benefits of refinancing. Execute LOANS30.EXE to run the program.

MortgageCalc calculates amortization tables, taking into consideration extra principle and balloon payments. Data can be exported to Excel, Lotus 1-2-3, and Quattro Pro formats. Run MORTSHAR.EXE from Windows. You can use the program for 30 days. (Copyright 1994, Leiphart Computing Services, Inc.)

Graphics, Worksheets, and Databases

On the CD you will also find graphics, worksheets, and databases illustrated in the text of the book. Access these following the same instructions as above. They will download to the chapter number to which they correspond. Here's what you'll find:

Worksheets

These worksheets are provided in both Excel (.XLS) and Lotus 1-2-3 (.WKS) formats:

ESTIM.XLS and **ESTIM.WKS** calculate materials needed for home improvement projects. Enter room measurements to calculate square feet of coverage and material requirements.

KITCHEN.XLS and **KITCHEN.WKS** help you budget and control home improvement projects. The worksheet maintains a running total of expenses and reports the amount remaining from your overall budget.

ELECEST.XLS and **ELECEST.WKS** calculate the cost of running electrical appliances. Enter information that you find on the appliances nameplate.

PLANTS.XLS and **PLANTS.WKS** help you organize your plants and garden. The worksheets are equivalent to databases also included on this CD.

NAMES.XLS and **NAMES.WKS** list the common and botanical names of 50 plants.

VENDORS.XLS and **VENDORS.WKS** let you track suppliers for plants and garden materials.

LOG.XLS and **LOG.WKS** let you maintain a log of your gardening activities and progress.

HOUSEHOL.XLS and **HOUSEHOL.WKS** let you maintain an inventory of your household possessions.

LOANQUAL.XLS and **LOANQUAL.WKS** help you determine if you qualify for a mortgage. Enter the income and expense details requested, along with the principle, rate, and length of the loan.

REFIN.XLS and **REFIN.WKS** will help you decide about refinancing your mortgage. Enter the information requested about your current mortgage and the proposed refinanced loan. The worksheet will report how your monthly payments and total interest will be affected.

Graphics

These graphic files are supplied on BMP format to open into Windows Paintbrush:
Electrical circuits:

→ SINGLE.BMP shows how to wire a light switch

→ THREEWAY.BMP shows how to wire a three-way switch

Kitchen and bath layouts:

→ WALLKIT.BMP shows a single wall kitchen layout

→ GALLEY.BMP illustrates a galley kitchen

→ L-KIT.BMP shows an L-shaped kitchen

→ U-KIT.BMP shows a U-shaped kitchen

→ WALLBATH.BMP illustrates a single wall bathroom

→ GALLEYB.BMP shows a galley bathroom

→ L-BATH.BMP shows an L-shaped bathroom

→ U-BATH.BMP presents a U-shaped bathroom

Databases

These databases are provided in both Access and dBase formats.

Microsoft Access Databases

PLANTS.MDB and **PLANTS.LDB** are a complete database for the gardener. They include tables for recording plants and suppliers and for maintaining your log. They also contain the common and botanical names for 50 plants.

HOMEINV.MDB and **HOMEINV.LDB** are a database for recording your home inventory.

dBase Formatted Databases

HOUSEHOL.DBF and **HOUSEHOL.DBT** maintain your household inventory.

LOG.DBF and **LOG.DBT** maintain a record of your gardening activities.

PLANTS.DBF maintains an inventory of your plants.

NAMES.DBF lists the common and botanical names of 50 plants.

VENDORS.DBF keeps track of your garden suppliers.

You will also find **DREAMBUY.DOC**, the Word for Windows document titled Financing and Finding Your Dream Home. Start Word and open the document.

Appendix B: *Where to Find It*

Below is a listing of home improvement software providers and their products.

4Home Productions (516) 342-2000	Simply House
Abracadata Ltd. (800) 541-4871	Design Your Own Home Landscape Design Your Own Home Interiors Design Your Own Home Architecture Sprout Design Estimator
Roger C. Altman 708 S. Ohio Avenue Davenport, IA 52802	Your Electrical Reference Source
Dennis E. Austin 493 Riverview Plainwell, Michigan 49080	Handyman Conversions
Autodesk (707) 794-1450	Autodesk Home Autodesk Landscape Autodesk Kitchen and Bath Autodesk Deck
Books That Work (800) 242-4546	Design and Build Your Deck Get Wired! Home Survival Toolkit 3D Landscape Homebuyer's Guide Home Repair Encyclopedia Building Materials Estimator Garden Plant Selector Landscape Backyard Construction Plumbing Essential Repairs Wiring Circuit Planner and Simulator

Broderbund Software, Inc. (800) 521-6263	3D Home Architect
Martin Butcher Box 58 Mbabane, Swaziland	MBWWYA.TXT and MBHTFA.TXT
Bruce Christensen 6594 Hudson Avenue Mentor, OH 44060-4545	X10XA3
CLAW Software P.O. Box 1000, 725 Morton Avenue Aurora, IL 60507-1000	Mini FEET INCH Dimensional Calculator
Computer Easy (800) 522-3279	3D Design Plus Estimator Plus FloorPlan Plus 3D
COSMI (301) 886-3510	3D Virtual Reality Roomplanner
CPR, Inc. P.O. Box 3465 Berkeley, CA 94703	Remodel Estimator
Deep River Publishing, Inc. (207) 871-1684	Complete House
Epsilon Computing 1668 Trillium Court Cincinnati, OH 45215	Design-A-Room
Expert Software (800) 759-2562	Expert Home Design
Foresight Software Company (800) 231-8574	Planix Home Architect Most Popular Home Designs
Larry E. Fosdick 2624 Whitman Drive Wilmington, DE 19808	X10CTL

FYI Software (203) 248-9991	Buying a Home
Jeff L. Gates P.O. Box 1561 Blaine, WA 98231	QualifyR Windows
GreenThumb Software (303) 499-1388	Land Designer
Bill Hammond 5714 N. I Street San Bernardino, CA 92407	Garden Companion
Home Plan Software 6890 Rimrock Valley Road Mountain Ranch, CA 95246	Home Plan
David Huras 37 Ruddell Crescent Georgetown, Ontario L7G 5N4 Canada	X10DC control
IEG Consultants P.O. Box 26931 San Jose, CA 95159	Smart Homeowner
Insight Software Solutions P.O. Box 354 Bountiful, UT 84011-0354	SmartTracker Inventory The Mortgage Analyser
IVI Publishing (800) 754-1484	Hometime Weekend Home Projects
Joy's Software P.O. Box 648 Marshall, MI 49068-0648	Hints and Tips
Kestrel Computing Company, Inc. P.O. Box 943 Denville, NJ 07834	House Mouse

Philip P. Kapusta P.O. Box 5423 Falmount, VA 22403	Home Loan Diary
Leiphart Computing Services, Inc. 1035 Hopewell Road Downingtown, PA 19335-1202	Mortgage Calc
MaeDae Enterprises 5430 Murr Road Peyton, CO 80831	Mortgage Designer
MultiCom (800) 850-7272	Better Homes and Gardens Complete Guide to Gardening
Don Norman Audit Planning Services 9411 Sandstone Avenue Houston, TX 77036	Master Amortiser
North Shore Home Inspections 3467 West 41st Street Cleveland, Ohio 44109	The Home Inspector
Ohio Star Software 8919 Deep Forest Lane Centerville, OH 45458	ANALYZ2 and AMORT.XLM
Ones & Zeros. Inc. (800) 882-2764	Per%Sense
Parsons Technology, Inc. (319) 395-9626	Home Buyer's Companion
Personal Vision, Inc. (800) 764-2235	Home Ownership Plus
Boyd W. Penn 91 Navarre Street Hyde Park, MA 02136	Automate

PSG HomeCraft Software P. O. Box 974 Tualatin, OR 97062	Multimedia Home Database Organize! Your Plants and Garden Organize! Your Home
Paul Postuma 16 Fullyer Drive Quispamis, NB, Canada E2g 1Y7	GrowEm
Red Poteet P.O. Box 548 587 F North Ventu Park Road Newbury Park, CA 91320	Red's Home Maintenance
RMH Computer Services P.O. Box 657 Beech Grove, IN 46107-0657	Around the House
Fred Schipp 1129 Hochgesang Avenue Jasper, IN 47546	Loan Arranger
Shannon Software, Ltd. (703) 573-9274	Gardener's Assistant (V.2.0)
Softkey (407) 367-0005	Key Home Designer
Sympathetic Software 9531 Telhan Drive Huntington Beach, CA 92646	Smart10
Sunrise Software 4821 Clydelle Avenue San Jose, CA 95124-4209	HortMan
Shapeware Software (800) 446-3335	Visio Home

INDEX

Ziff-Davis Press Survey of Readers

Please help us in our effort to produce the best books on personal computing.
For your assistance, we would be pleased to send you a FREE catalog
featuring the complete line of Ziff-Davis Press books.

1. How did you first learn about this book?

Recommended by a friend . . . . ☐ -1 (5)

Recommended by store personnel . . . . ☐ -2

Saw in Ziff-Davis Press catalog . . . . ☐ -3

Received advertisement in the mail . . . . ☐ -4

Saw the book on bookshelf at store . . . . ☐ -5

Read book review in: _____ ☐ -6

Saw an advertisement in: _____ ☐ -7

Other (Please specify): _____ ☐ -8

2. Which THREE of the following factors most influenced your decision to purchase this book? (Please check up to THREE.)

Front or back cover information on book . . . ☐ -1 (6)

Logo of magazine affiliated with book . . . . . . ☐ -2

Special approach to the content . . . . ☐ -3

Completeness of content . . . . ☐ -4

Author's reputation. ☐ -5

Publisher's reputation . . . . ☐ -6

Book cover design or layout . . . . ☐ -7

Index or table of contents of book . . . . ☐ -8

Price of book . . . . ☐ -9

Special effects, graphics, illustrations . . . . . . ☐ -0

Other (Please specify): _____ ☐ -x

3. How many computer books have you purchased in the last six months? _____ (7-10)

4. On a scale of 1 to 5, where 5 is excellent, 4 is above average, 3 is average, 2 is below average, and 1 is poor, please rate each of the following aspects of this book below. (Please circle your answer.)

Depth/completeness of coverage   5 4 3 2 1 (11)

Organization of material   5 4 3 2 1 (12)

Ease of finding topic   5 4 3 2 1 (13)

Special features/time saving tips 5 4 3 2 1 (14)

Appropriate level of writing   5 4 3 2 1 (15)

Usefulness of table of contents   5 4 3 2 1 (16)

Usefulness of index   5 4 3 2 1 (17)

Usefulness of accompanying disk   5 4 3 2 1 (18)

Usefulness of illustrations/graphics 5 4 3 2 1 (19)

Cover design and attractiveness   5 4 3 2 1 (20)

Overall design and layout of book 5 4 3 2 1 (21)

Overall satisfaction with book   5 4 3 2 1 (22)

5. Which of the following computer publications do you read regularly; that is, 3 out of 4 issues?

Byte . . . . ☐ -1 (23)

Computer Shopper . . . . ☐ -2

Home Office Computing . . . . ☐ -3

Dr. Dobb's Journal . . . . ☐ -4

LAN Magazine . . . . ☐ -5

MacWEEK . . . . ☐ -6

MacUser . . . . ☐ -7

PC Computing . . . . ☐ -8

PC Magazine . . . . ☐ -9

PC WEEK . . . . ☐ -0

Windows Sources . . . . ☐ -x

Other (Please specify): _____ ☐ -y

Please turn page.

6. What is your level of experience with personal computers? With the subject of this book?

	With PCs	With subject of book
Beginner	☐ -1 (24)	☐ -1 (25)
Intermediate	☐ -2	☐ -2
Advanced	☐ -3	☐ -3

7. Which of the following best describes your job title?

Officer (CEO/President/VP/owner)....... ☐ -1 (26)
Director/head............................ ☐ -2
Manager/supervisor...................... ☐ -3
Administration/staff..................... ☐ -4
Teacher/educator/trainer................. ☐ -5
Lawyer/doctor/medical professional....... ☐ -6
Engineer/technician...................... ☐ -7
Consultant............................... ☐ -8
Not employed/student/retired............. ☐ -9
Other (Please specify): _____ ☐ -0

8. What is your age?

Under 20............................ ☐ -1 (27)
21-29.............................. ☐ -2
30-39.............................. ☐ -3
40-49.............................. ☐ -4
50-59.............................. ☐ -5
60 or over......................... ☐ -6

9. Are you:

Male............................... ☐ -1 (28)
Female............................. ☐ -2

Thank you for your assistance with this important information! Please write your address below to receive our free catalog.

Name: _____

Address: _____

City/State/Zip: _____

Fold here to mail.

3342-16-20